INCREASING RETAILER PRODUCTIVITY

A GUIDE FOR SHOPPING CENTER PROFESSIONALS

International Council of Shopping Centers

New York

Published by
International Council of Shopping Centers
Publications Department
665 Fifth Avenue
New York, NY 10022

Text Design by: H. Roberts
Cover Design by: Richard Rossiter

ICSC Catalog Number: 852

Library of Congress Cataloging-in-Publication Data

Increasing Retailer Productivity: A Guide for Shopping Center Professionals

Bibliography: p.
1. Shopping centers—Management.   2. Shopping centers—Marketing.   3. Retail trade—Management.
I. International Council of Shopping Centers.
HF5430.S557   1988   658.8'7   87-22546
ISBN 0-913598-73-9 (pbk.)

Printed in the U.S.A.

Contents

Foreword

Today's retail business is not for the faint of heart. Complexities abound.

Customer demands are growing, while market niches are multiplying and becoming increasingly selective. Changes in taste, style, and shopping habits are cropping up faster than ever, making today's hard-and-fast rules tomorrow's outworn ideas.

Yet, even as it becomes harder to evaluate trends and stay a step ahead, retailing continues to attract people who are among the most daring and creative in the business world. The vitality these retailers bring to a shopping center is a precious asset.

Nonetheless, shopping center professionals, with their industry-wide perspective and problem-solving expertise, can be of great help to the retailer. They can help ensure that whether a store is thriving or struggling, the fundamental principles of the business—merchandise assortment, visual presentation, financial planning, customer service, and advertising/promotion—are not neglected. For today's retailer, prospects for success will always hinge upon adherence to the fundamentals.

The contributors to this book are among today's leading professional retail consultants. While you may be familiar with much of the wisdom they've written on these pages, there are countless ideas here that will be new to you. So read on and enjoy this unique ICSC volume. You'll find it enormously helpful and a timely reminder that only through learning and changing can we stay on top of today's retailing.

Barbara Ashley
Vice President, Retail Analysis
The Taubman Company, Inc.

Preface

As a shopping center owner/developer, manager, marketing director or other shopping center professional, you have a vested interest in the productivity and profitability of your retail tenants. However, when your retailers encounter problems, you may find that despite the lack of a retailing background, you are in the best position to help your tenants and increase the productivity of your center.

Increasing Retailer Productivity: A Guide for Shopping Center Professionals provides retailing techniques that can help you help your tenants. It shows you how to:

- create exciting visual merchandising displays through improved signage, lighting, floor, wall and window displays, and color.
- use market demographics to draw the right customers into the store at the right time.
- increase profits by better budgeting and forecasting of retail financial data, including inventory, pricing and purchasing information.
- develop effective store advertising and promotional campaigns.
- improve selling skills and customer service.

Included is a Resources directory that provides a listing of retail-oriented consultants, trade organizations, publications, audiovisuals, meetings, conventions and trade shows where you can get additional expert information and assistance. Other chapters discuss how to find and work with retail consultants and how to motivate merchant participation in center-sponsored retail-assistance activities.

This book does not attempt to make you an expert in all aspects of retailing. It is designed to provide you with enough retailing know-how to identify tenants in trouble. It is also full of ideas on how you can reach out to the merchants in your center and work with them to increase productivity and sales.

Acknowledgments

This publication is based on interviews with and information submitted by shopping center managers, marketing directors, and consultants. Grateful acknowledgment is made to the following individuals and companies who have contributed information to the International Council of Shopping Centers and this publication:

Karen Aboussie, CMD, is assistant vice president and director of corporate marketing for Goodman Segar Hogan, Inc., a commercial real estate company in Virginia which manages 15,615,000 square feet of shopping space ranging from strip centers to super regionals. Ms. Aboussie is a member of the International Council of Shopping Centers' Certified Shopping Center Manager/Certified Marketing Director Commission and speaks frequently at ICSC marketing conferences.

Barbara Ashley is vice president retail analysis for The Taubman Company, Inc., a real estate development and property management firm located in Bloomfield Hills, Michigan, which has created more than 75 million square feet of commercial and mixed-use properties. Prior to joining The Taubman Company in 1987, Ms. Ashley worked as a buyer for Bloomingdale's and subsequently operated a private retail consulting firm for five years.

Kenneth A. Banks is vice president for marketing communications for Eckerd Drug Company, a Florida-based chain with stores in shopping malls. Eckerd won the *Advertising Age* award for the top TV retail commercials in 1984 and 1985, Retail Advertising Conference awards for both TV and radio in 1985 and 1986, and the top campaign award at the International Film Festival in New York City in 1987.

W. Edward Brandon, CSM, is president of the Brandon Company, Miami, Florida, which owns 10 shopping centers, each with fewer than 200,000 square feet gross leasable area and 50–70 tenants, 95% of which are "mom-and-pop" stores. Mr. Brandon is a trustee of the International Council of Shopping Centers. He was the chairman of ICSC's Insurance Committee and is now vice president, Committees.

Liz Coleman-Napoli, CMD, is the general manager of Riverside Square, a JMB/Federated Realty center in Hackensack, New Jersey, with more than 90 fashion stores and restaurants. Ms. Coleman-Napoli has been a member of the International Council of Shopping Centers' Certified Marketing Director Committee and is a past chair of the organization's Eastern States Marketing Conference.

Edie Crane, CMD, is vice president of marketing for David Hocker & Associates in Owensboro, Kentucky, which has developed 30 centers containing 7 million square feet of shopping space. Edie Crane has had extensive experience establishing and supervising marketing programs which include motivational and incentive programs.

Richard Echikson is chairman of Retail Consultants, Inc. in Millburn, New Jersey, which provides consulting services to guide center owners. Mr. Echikson has been a speaker at International Council of Shopping Centers' conferences and Idea Exchanges, and is a faculty member of the International Council of Shopping Centers University of Shopping Centers, where he conducts a course entitled "Helping Merchants Help Themselves."

Charlotte Ellis, CMD, is vice president of marketing for Lehndorff USA group of companies in Dallas, Texas. Since 1974, she has been involved in shopping center marketing and advertising. She is currently responsible for the marketing programs of Lehndorff's nine regional centers, 13 community centers, 36 office buildings, as well as the company's corporate advertising and public relations. She has also served on the faculty of International Council of Shopping Centers' Marketing Institute.

Robert M. Jones, CMD, is a principal in Stillerman Jones & Company, Inc., of Indianapolis, Indiana, an international shopping center and retail services firm which specializes in management, marketing research and leasing. Mr. Jones is a frequent instructor at International Council of Shopping Centers' institutes and has served on the Admissions and Governing Committee for the Certified Marketing Director professional designation.

Betty Konarski has spent 15 years as retail store owner and shopping center manager. She is currently dividing her time between consulting with mall developers in Washington and Oregon and supervising the Small Business Institute at Seattle University, Seattle, Washington.

Rebecca L. Maccardini, CMD, is director of operations for Forbes/Cohen Properties, Southfield, Michigan, which operates three regional centers in middle markets. Ms. Maccardini became, in 1980, a trustee of the International Council of Shopping Centers. In 1981 she was elected divisional vice president for the Midwest Division and in 1982 vice president of committees of the International Council of Shopping Centers, a position to which she was reelected in 1983 and 1984. She is currently chairman of the International Council of Shopping Centers' Committee on Professional Development and serves on the advisory board of *Shopping Center World* magazine.

Pamela Muston is a retail consultant at Melvin Simon & Associates, Inc., an Indianapolis-based real estate developer. The firm manages 60 million square feet of space in 39 states and is one of the largest shopping center developers, with 130 shopping facilities in 25 states. Prior to joining Melvin Simon & Associates in 1985, Ms. Muston worked for a national junior specialty chain for 15 years.

Karen Samford is corporate marketing manager for Herring Marathon Group, Dallas, Texas, a firm specializing in an analytical approach to its marketing. She has been in the shopping center industry for 7 years, is a former MAXI award winner, and conducted a 1987 International Council of Shopping Centers' Fall Conference session on marketing a group of centers as a package.

Jane A. Secola, CMD, past member of the International Council of Shopping Centers' Certified Marketing Director Committee, was project coordinator for the first public service program offered by the International Council of Shopping Centers (ICSC), the KIDS program in 1986. She has spoken at many ICSC panels and workshops, and is the winner of many ICSC awards, including the first MAXI award for merchant motivation with the quality circle concept. She is presently working as a marketing specialist and strategist for retail shopping centers.

Garnet Vaughan Smith, CMD, is director of marketing for The RREEF Funds, a closed-end real estate equity investments management firm for pension plans. She is on the International Council of Shopping Centers' MAXI Screening Committee and is the CMD Subcommittee Chairman for the CSM/CMD Commissions. She is also an instructor with the ICSC Marketing Institute.

Ann Taradash is vice president for leasing and marketing at the Century Shopping Centre, Chicago, Illinois.

Joseph Weishar is the president and founder of New Vision Studios, Inc. in New York City. He has spoken at both national and regional International Council of Shopping Centers conferences and has consulted for individual companies which are members of International Council of Shopping Centers. He teaches merchandise presentation at the Fashion Institute of Technology in New York, and writes a regular column on visual merchandising for *Visual Merchandising and Store Design* magazine.

John Williams is president of John C. Williams Consultants Ltd., a Canadian retail marketing, planning, and market research company which, in addition to other activities, provides shopping center developers with retail workshops, merchant counseling, advice on merchant mix, and marketing plans. Mr. Williams is a member of the International Council of Shopping Centers and has spoken at the organization's conventions. He is coauthor of the National Retail Merchants Association's and Retail Council of Canada's *Strategic Retail Marketing—How to Be a Winner* and *Christmas Planning & Ideas* workbooks.

Carol L. Zimmer is the corporate marketing director for Forbes/Cohen Properties, Southfield, Michigan. Recently promoted, Ms. Zimmer began her shopping center career with Forbes/Cohen as marketing diector of the Lansing Mall, a regional center with 125 stores in Lansing, Michigan.

1

Talking to Retailers: How the Experts Do It

- **W. Edward Brandon, CSM,** The Brandon Co.

- **Rebecca L. Maccardini, CMD,** Forbes/Cohen Properties

- **Garnet Vaughan Smith, CMD,** The RREEF Funds

- **Ann Taradash,** The Century Shopping Centre

Recognizing that it is not always easy for center management to approach merchants, ICSC brought together a panel of shopping center experts to ascertain their ideas on how to work with retailers. A transcript of the panel discussion follows.

ICSC: *Why should center management spend time and effort helping retailers?*
Brandon: We want merchants to succeed. They're our bread and butter. If a merchant fails, it's our failure. It hurts us in future leasing, in managing the remaining stores, and in marketing and promoting the center. It's a black mark that casts a shadow over the entire operation. And it injures our pride.

A distinction needs to be drawn, however, between a small center and a large mall. The small center operator needs to spend much more time and effort helping retailers than seems to be true in the larger ones. Small centers have more "moms and pops" and merchants who may be relatively unsophisticated about retailing. Helping retailers in small centers can pose problems and challenges for developers that were virtually unthought-of ten years ago.

Maccardini: We should help retailers because successful stores produce percentage rent, whereas unsuccessful stores go black and we lose even the minimum rent. Also, I have found that some of the most rewarding moments in our job come from the feeling that we have helped a retailer—and also ourselves.

Smith: The management team should spend time and effort helping retailers because success breeds success. Successful retail means fully leased centers—and that's critical. Vacancies project a negative image to your customers, your existing merchants, and your prospective merchants.

ICSC: *What is the role of center management in communicating with retailers about improving their stores?*

Taradash: We should be thought of by retailers as part of their team, someone on their side. Center managers should not expect to become retail experts. They need, however, enough knowledge in different areas so they can spot problems even before the sales figures are in and, as part of a cooperative process, bring them tactfully to the attention of store managers. With very little expertise, a center manager should be able to notice when merchandise is old or out of style and when a display is poorly arranged or poorly lit or hasn't been changed in many weeks. If a small store is trying to be all things to all people, center management should notice the lack of focus and ask the retailer to do some self-examination.

The center management staff must also be center shoppers, and learn to think like customers. Center managers must concentrate on the psychology of buying, not that of selling. Seeing things as the customer sees them and being able to relate that tactfully to the retailer is an invaluable skill.

Once the merchant agrees to take the advice given and work on a problem, the center management's next task is to suggest local experts who can help in the following areas:

- Local advertising and public relations agencies.
- Visual merchandisers—usually display people from local department stores.
- Retail consultants who can help with merchandising, personnel management, operational systems, financial planning, and financial systems.

Smith: The role of center management is to analyze the situation, identify problems and opportunities, and set measurable objectives. Once this is done, a strategy can be formulated and acted upon. For example, small centers without on-site management professionals can hire a specialized consultant to conduct a retail enhancement program. When done right, this step conveys caring and concern to the merchants. It says: "We're not ignoring you. We think bringing in an outside expert may help because . . ." The approach, however, must be sincere, and the objectives well communicated. To do it right means having the right intentions and communicating them in the right way. You won't fool the merchants with a one-shot attempt at support. Your efforts must be consistent and sincere. The merchants must understand the good business reasons for conducting the program so they can make a commitment to participate and follow through on suggestions.

Maccardini: I agree that once we are better educated about retailing, our role is primarily to identify problems, not to solve them. Very few of us in the operations end of the shopping center industry are proficient enough at retailing to become retail consultants. Identifying problem areas, motivating merchants, and getting them together with proper consultants can be the best service we can render. In fact, the ability to identify the problem early is something center management and marketing should concentrate on. If the problem is not identified early enough, the merchant may in many cases not even have enough working capital left to correct it. And remember, consultants are not always necessarily expensive. There are low-cost and even no-cost consultants. Newspapers, for example, often offer consultation about advertising. Universities have courses on retailing, and other retailers can be a helpful source for the less sophisticated merchant.

Brandon: In my experience, having a high-priced retail consultant come to the center for a day is not the right approach to solving the basic problems that smaller centers face. To begin with, the cost is generally prohibitive. You can't afford that sort of treatment often enough to impact on enough people and justify the per-person cost.

We need to develop techniques that will allow the developer, manager, or marketing director to conduct small groups several times a year to teach retail techniques. The merchants in these centers may be naive, but they want to succeed. Their future is in the hands of minimum-wage sales personnel, either part-time or full-time, so that employee turnover is high and loyalty thin. They would benefit greatly from, say, one-hour group sessions built around a set of video tapes that address selling skills, visual merchandising, buying, fiscal management, client-list use, and advertising and promotion. Each tape should be 15 to 20 minutes in length and be backed up by discussion-guide materials.

Basically, we have to meet the retailers at the level of their needs. We have to energize, encourage, and motivate them, but with a touch of tender loving care. Retailers are just like anybody else: they want human warmth and recognition. We have to become more humanitarian in our approach, by maintaining an achievable set of standards.

ICSC: *What do you see as the role of the center's marketing director in approaching retailers to help improve performance?*

Smith: The marketing director's advice and support should be a thread that runs through center management's approach to merchant relations. There must be day-to-day attention given to initiating and building relationships. Once-a-month conversations at a meeting just won't suffice. Marketing directors must help the retailers—and sometimes even the center management team—understand what an important resource the marketing director can be.

The marketing director should be visible—and I don't

mean just walking the mall. Store visits should be regular and meaningful, with conversations a combination of information and motivation.

It's easy to develop a marketing plan in a vacuum, but that plan probably won't accomplish much on its own. Its success depends upon the relationships with the merchants. Developing and building those relationships can be a challenge—just keeping up with the changing players is part of it—but it's a challenge that must be met and made a priority.

Maccardini: A developer or mall manager must make good use of the marketing director, who probably has more knowledge than the center manager about such things as visual merchandising, fashion, advertising, current trends, and local market demographics. This means structuring the marketing director's job in such a way that time is available to work with merchants. It might also mean additional personnel on the marketing staff or some joint involvement by the center manager.

ICSC: *Given that resources and time are limited, which stores should be approached with retailing help?*

Taradash: National chains will not generally be receptive to advice. Even though many local stores seem to have "tunnel vision," they are generally more receptive to help and the results are more rewarding. Our approach has been to select a store that obviously needed some merchandising expertise and create a new look for it resulting in improved sales. Their success then served as an example to the other stores. This kind of starting point creates credibility with the other merchants and gives center management an opening for continuing the process with other stores, especially those that are near percentage rent and are vital to the merchandise mix of the center.

Maccardini: Even national chains will respond if the approach is right and you go through the right channels and reach the right people. I advise center managers and marketing directors to select stores on the basis of where they feel they will get the most response and where their efforts will produce the most in terms of sales increases and percentage rent generated.

We go after three groups:

1. Stores that are producing percentage rent.
2. Stores that are very close to percentage rent; since they are doing well, they require special expertise to understand how they can do better.
3. Troubled stores in danger of going under that we want to keep, because they have a good local name or we need them for merchant mix.

A vacant store means no rent at all for three to six months, which we want to avoid if possible. With all the center manager and marketing director have to do, it is hard to find energy and time for stores that do not fall into these categories.

A center manager should also step in when obvious problems occur, such as a store manager spending an excessive amount of time outside the store, a store continually opening late or closing early, empty shelves creating inventory problems, or other in-store problems that threaten sales success. Then it is necessary to go over the store manager's head, and get the problem rectified.

Brandon: I believe we should have an ongoing relationship with all of our retailers, not just the troubled ones. We should know how the successful stores achieved their success, so we can use them as role models for the weak and weary.

Our efforts are aimed at exploiting the successes of our better merchants and at undergirding the weaker ones by any means available. In smaller centers, the available resources and the steps that can be taken are much more limited than in a regional mall. The key to spending time with the weaker merchants is recognizing the point at which it is a hopeless case. Too often, we keep merchants in business when we should not, doing neither them nor ourselves a favor.

Smith: I look first at the stores with overage potential. What are these folks doing right, and what can we do to help them do it better? There's often a tendency to focus on the store in deepest trouble. But that trouble may be something you can't help. The store may be undercapitalized. Customer service could be weak, sales training poor, store design inefficient, or the store could just be in the wrong space at the wrong time.

Choosing the merchants we will help must be more than a good neighbor decision—it must be a good business decision. What is your objective? To push the store into percentage rent? To save the store from bankruptcy? To minimize the risk and end the relationship? Clearly identifying your goals will guide your actions.

If an entire category is not doing well or an area of the mall shows weakness, there may be a bigger problem. The situation should be carefully researched and analyzed so a plan can be developed to rectify the situation.

ICSC: *Who in the store should be approached?*
Maccardini: Most of the time it's simple to decide: You approach the store manager. If the owner is also the manager and is willing to listen, that's your best bet. But once you're talking about a multistore operation, it's not always so obvious. We have a store audit form, which asks where the authority is. For instance, it asks who has the authority to:

- Move merchandise around.
- Do markdowns.
- Do signage.
- Merchandise.
- Hire salespeople.
- Train salespeople.

I suggest not going in with the form but just questioning, maybe over several visits, who can do what. Once you know where the authority is, go to the person who can actually bring about change in the problem area. This may be someone two or three levels above the store manager. Even where the store manager is technically in charge, it may be necessary to go higher if that person is not doing a good job. Another reason to go above the store level is if a chain of stores does poorly in several of your centers. You should then be dealing with the corporate office.

ICSC: *Many retailers and center managers think of their relationship with each other as adversarial rather than advisory. Given that history, how should center managers approach retailers?*

Smith: Managers should approach their retailers with a positive attitude, an open mind and a desire to help. Regardless of how adversarial your merchant relationships might have been, put the past aside so you can work together toward the common goal. Concentrate on being constructive instead of critical. Work with your merchants as peers. Ask questions which lead them to the right decision on their own. Make a commitment to communication that helps develop relationships.

Mall policy issues, such as employee parking, can create controversy, but they can also provide oppportunities for positive communication. Take the time to explain how the mall's policies contribute toward a pleasant shopping experience. Instead of criticizing, offer assistance. If a policy prohibits taping signs to store windows and a merchant uses taped signs, suggest, "Dowel rods work well for hanging signs," and provide the needed rods. An expense, yes, but a small price to pay to correct a problem and create an environment conducive to team problem solving.

Brandon: We need to approach retailers on an ongoing basis with an air of helpfulness and not as if we were starting an inquisition. Our contact with merchants shouldn't be just at those times when negative circumstances are involved, such as collecting rents or enforcing store hours. Create positive conditions and praise the merchant wherever possible, even if the conversation winds up with an attempt to restructure the merchant's attitude.

We need to know enough about the retailer and the individual business to speak the same language—not just lease-enforcement language. Be sympathetic to the merchant's problems. With some, the therapy approach will help; with others, small talk is a good start, beginning with concern for the merchant's family and leading up to "What can I do to help you?"

Maccardini: We have a fairly structured program in which we ask center management to develop a plan with the targeted store managers. But I suggest approaching the store-level person informally, engaging in a conversation—with no paper and pencil—about the future. Getting the store person involved in making a plan is key. Asking some of the following kinds of questions gets them thinking, and their answers will actually help formulate the plan you will follow.

- What are your personal goals regarding the store?
- What percentage increase in sales are you trying to achieve this month? This year?
- Are there any special company incentives you are trying to achieve this year?
- Are there any special incentives you can give your employees for doing outstanding sales? Maybe we can think of some.
- If the store is outdated, where are you on the store remodel list? Why don't we work together to see if we can get you moved up?
- Let's review the mall program and see if there are any special ways your store might benefit from it.
- How can I help you achieve your goals?

An initial conversation based on these questions opens the door to other conversations, in which you refer to the merchants' goals.

In some cases, if the situation is obviously bad and you feel a direct approach might work, you can say, "I see we've got a problem with . . . Let's talk about solutions and approaches to solving it." You can also say, "You've been picked for your potential," then help the store develop a plan. If the store is part of a chain, the plan may involve speaking to people beyond the store manager. Just make sure the merchants know you're interested in what they're doing, not in dictating to them.

In your dealings with retailers, ask a lot and tell little. It's amazing what people reveal that will let you help them. Just remember, about the only bad thing that can happen is that someone will not want your help. If you're not afraid of having someone say to you, "It's none of your business," there's nothing that can stop you from working with a store and finding out what is really wrong and what is really needed.

ICSC: *What types of suggestions can center managers make most easily?*

Smith: I really believe that the ease of making suggestions relates more to the people who are involved in making and accepting a suggestion than it does to the type of suggestion being made. When the relationship with your retailer is built on respect and trust, any type of suggestion should be easy. Then it's simply a question of presenting your idea to the right person, in the right way, at the right time, and in the right place.

ICSC: *What kind of program have you run with retailers?*

Maccardini: Forbes/Cohen has a structured program aimed at creating more overage rent. We call it the Target Store Program. Although the program comes from our corporate office, we rely on center managers and marketing directors to carry it out. The program has eight steps:

1. Classify each store in the center as either "good," "medium," or "in danger" via a store audit and review of sales figures.
2. Choose the stores where center management can be most helpful, based on a good relationship with the store manager or personal knowledge of the business.
3. Spell out for the developer or corporate headquarters why the stores have been selected.
4. Develop a plan for helping the stores, including a projection of expected gain and steps to take to help achieve them. This is where the initial approach to the store manager with questions about goals, discussed earlier, comes in.
5. Watch monthly sales figures carefully to see how they compare to your projections. Discuss major increases or decreases immediately with the stores.
6. Keep a diary of store visits, results, and expected future action.
7. Update the diary and the plan quarterly.
8. At the end of the year, analyze what has been accomplished based on the goals you set.

We have periodic joint meetings involving all the centers in which each center manager and marketing director reports on their most successful efforts in the program. This keeps everyone actively aware of the program and enables them to learn from each other. Retail consultants are sometimes brought in for this meeting, and representatives from our stores are asked to talk about how they are structured and how merchandise moves through their system. This gives our own mall personnel an opportunity to understand different structures as well as to form closer relationships with individual merchants.

ICSC: *What is your role, as director of operations for Forbes/ Cohen, in this program?*
Maccardini: I review the store choices and plans of the center's marketing director and manager. We make changes together where appropriate. Additionally, I monitor their progress through forms and meetings. I also attempt to put them in learning situations from time to time via speakers, ICSC programs, and other forms of education. This year, we began a more active corporate program which follows up where the marketing director and center manager leave off; this program takes on certain stores as a group, and generally lends support and backup for the overall program.

If the program produces verifiable results, I hope to be in the position of rewarding successful center managers and marketing directors financially for their work with retailers — but the program must mature before that can happen.

ICSC: *How has the program worked?*
Maccardini: In a few cases, it enhanced percentage rent. In a couple of cases, it led retailers to reevaluate their merchandise mix, which should produce better future results. In one or two cases, it actually caused us to reevaluate the merchant and make some decisions, including buying out a store's lease. Certainly, it has made the marketing directors and managers more aware of what is happening and more sensitive to planning programs that are relevant to the stores' needs and problems.

ICSC: *Why hasn't the program been more successful?*
Maccardini: There are several reasons:

1. My people are very busy with their traditional center responsibilities.
2. Some are uncomfortable with their knowledge of retailing.
3. If not handled correctly, the retailers resist the program.

ICSC: *How do you deal with these problems?*
Maccardini: I tell center managers who are insecure about their retail knowledge to concentrate on what they do know, such as the physical condition of a store—remodeling, cleanliness, etc.—and the co-op advertising program. I encourage them at the very least to be the "squeaky wheel," by, for example, pointing out that "in such-and-such a category (say, shoes) your sales rank is —— and this means you may need some help." Sometimes it's the center management's job to report problems to the district store manager, saying, "Your store manager is never in the store and I think you may have a management problem there."

ICSC: *I understand that at the Century Shopping Centre the approach is different.*
Taradash: At Century, our approach is a little less formal and more personal, one-on-one. It is somewhat easier to establish that personal level at a smaller specialty center. An excellent way to break the ice is to offer to help a store that center management staff agrees needs considerable help in merchandising. This involves explaining the mall's target market, supporting your explanation with research, and showing the merchant how the store could better serve the target market by taking advantage of help from center management or from an outside retail expert—free of charge.

We recently had a success story. We selected one of our stores that needed considerable improvement both visually and in sales, and said, "We plan to change the image and merchandise direction of the center, and we feel your store could benefit from some changes that would be in keeping with the new image. Let's begin by creating an area in your store that will appeal to the customers we're targeting."

At first the merchant was resistant, but an "It-can't-hurt-to-try" enthusiastic attitude won him over. I showed up in blue jeans and spent a week with the merchant re-doing the store, arranging the merchandise so it made a statement by type, by color, and so on. (If I had not been qualified in this area, I would have hired someone from the outside.) In two months, sales doubled and within a year, they tripled. These people now own three stores in the mall; they have become very cooperative and are an example to other merchants who need to make changes. Before they opened their newest store, one for children, I was able to get them to hire outside retail consultants.

From that initial effort, we gained credibility with the other merchants, who are now more open to our suggestions and help on an ongoing basis. In fact, we have helped remerchandise, reposition, and redesign several stores in our center with great success—and increased sales levels. We have also hired a retail consultant who comes to the center once a month and makes appointments with stores that need help with visual merchandising, customer relations, or promotional ideas. The stores look forward to this one-on-one visit and feel the consultant is on their team.

ICSC: *How can merchants learn from each other?*
Brandon: It is probably common to both regional and small centers that merchants aren't inclined to be overly helpful to one another. In general, the community spirit that should be there, isn't. The reality is that the average person is both selfish and egocentric.

It is, therefore, a pleasure to find merchants who are willing to share their professionalism with others. Where this occurs, you should take advantage of the availability, yet use them with caution. Almost everything any merchant knows is something that was learned from another merchant, but no merchant wants to be too obviously force-fed.
Smith: It's a big challenge. There's a lot of ego involved and merchants are not always willing to share; after all, they are still competitors. Success is contagious, true, yet it's difficult for them to accept the concept when their prime consideration

is the bottom line. Cross-merchandising programs can open the door and get merchants talking to one another. Then the results can speak for themselves.

Maccardini: That is not a key part of most programs, and you cannot expect a lot in this area. However, in category meetings merchants may discuss in general terms what will help in that category, such as mallwide promotions, clinics, or giveaways.

ICSC: *What are some possible pitfalls of a program for communicating with retailers?*

Brandon: The centuries-old adversarial relationship between landlord and tenant colors every contact and conversation with retailers in one way or another. One pitfall is to ignore that fact. This adversarial character can combine with the partnership aspect to make the relationship a bittersweet one. To ignore retailers, to communicate too little or to speak down to them, can all be serious communication pitfalls. The approach to a merchant by a landlord or an agent, whether by management or by marketing, should be on as nearly an equal basis as possible. Self-respect and dignity should always be preserved.

There are times, however, when the center manager must maintain a hard line and preserve the center's rights under the agreement between landlord and retailer. At this point, equality ceases and legal correctness prevails. Knowing how to balance the negatives and positives of the relationship is the essence of our professional goals.

Maccardini: One of the biggest pitfalls is not understanding the individual stores and their structures and where decisions are made within the company. You must learn how much authority the on-site store manager has.

Another problem is working out the proper approach to the retailer. If you say, "I'm going to help you run your business," you will get nowhere. However, if you involve the retailer from the beginning with a "How can we do this together?" attitude, you'll have a better chance of success.

Smith: Some of the problems with programs for communicating with retailers stem from lack of believability and trust. If the merchants question your motives, you'll have problems. They must have a clear understanding of your objectives.

Explain what's in it for them and be frank about what's in it for you. In both cases there's one aim—success!

You also have to be careful when your suggested changes require additional expense. If the store spends time and money trying to change and your plan doesn't work, you'll have a new problem on your hands. One way to avoid this outcome is to concentrate your time and talent on those retailers with the greatest potential for success. Make sure you're planning a win-win situation.

ICSC: *What if a retailer will not take your advice?*
Smith: If the retailer doesn't want to take your advice, then you have to do three things:

1. Reexamine your suggestions. Are you absolutely right? Does the approach need refinement? Did you address the most critical issues?
2. If your evaluation is correct, is your solution feasible? Does the merchant have the resources to effect the change? Is the money available? Is there corporate support? Do the people involved have the necessary knowledge and skills to generate results?
3. If you answer yes to everything, take a look at your means of communicating the idea. You may not have made yourself clear. Or you may have gotten your point across, but to the wrong person, or to the right person in the wrong tone of voice.

If your evaluation is accurate, your strategy sound, and your suggestions feasible, yet the retailer still won't take your advice, then the manager doesn't understand the good business reasons for accepting your suggestions or, has made the conscious decision, for whatever reason, not to take advantage of your input. In either case, if at first you don't succeed . . .
Maccardini: While you cannot insist on anything that is not in the lease, you definitely have some additional leverage as a lease approaches renewal time. For the most part, however, attempting to make your comments and questions relevant to retailers' needs is imperative if you expect to get any results.

Smith: Our relationship with our merchants is a two-way street. Spell it out: if they do well, we do well; and, if we do well, they do well. That's a win-win situation, just plain good business.

W. Edward Brandon, CSM, is president of the Brandon Company, Miami, Florida, which owns 10 shopping centers, each with fewer than 200,000 square feet gross leasable area, and 50–70 tenants, 95% of which are "mom and pop" stores. Mr. Brandon is a trustee of the International Council of Shopping Centers. He was the chairman of ICSC's Insurance Committee and is now vice president, Committees.

Rebecca L. Maccardini, CMD, is director of operations for Forbes/Cohen Properties, Southfield, Michigan, which operates three regional centers in Michigan and Florida. Ms. Maccardini became, in 1980, a trustee of the International Council of Shopping Centers. Ms. Maccardini chaired the CMD Committee for 3 years and has taught in both the Management and Marketing Institutes for the ICSC. In 1981 she was elected divisional vice president for the Midwest Division and in 1982 vice president of committees of the International Council of Shopping Centers, a position to which she was reelected in 1983 and 1984. She is currently chairman of the ICSC Committee on Professional Development and serves on the advisory board of *Shopping Center World* magazine.

Garnet Vaughan Smith, CMD, is director of marketing for The RREEF Funds, a closed-end real estate equity investments management firm for pension plans. She is on the International Council of Shopping Centers' MAXI Screening Committee and is the CMD Subcommittee Chairman for the CSM/CMD Commissions. She is also an instructor with the ICSC Marketing Institute.

Ann Taradash is vice president for leasing and marketing at the Century Shopping Centre, Chicago, Illinois.

2

Retail Consultants: Finding One, Working With One

- Karen Aboussie, CMD, Goodman Segar Hogan, Inc.
- Richard Echikson, Retail Consultants, Inc.

Bringing in a retail consultant is one way developers can help the merchants in their centers. In order to help its members make the most effective use of an outside expert, the International Council of Shopping Centers (ICSC) asked Richard Echikson, chairman of Retail Consultants in New Jersey, and Karen Aboussie, CMD, of Goodman Segar Hogan in Virginia, which uses consultants, for some tips on how to utilize a consultant's services most productively. Instead of disagreement between the buyer and seller of expertise, we found differences in emphasis, which together give a complete picture of the process of working with a retail consultant.

ICSC: *How should a center or developer choose a consultant?*
Aboussie: First analyze your situation and determine your specific goals. Research will probably lead you to one or several of the four following areas:

- Store management and employees.
- Consumers.
- Sales.
- Special situation of the center.

In evaluating store management and employees, find out if your merchants are having trouble maintaining a staff. Do the merchants have access to a good corporate training program on specific selling techniques? Do the merchants seem apathetic? Do they have incentives for good performance, such as internal rewards or competitions?

Determine the strengths and weaknesses of your center and stores as perceived by the consumer. (Note that these will be perceptions, which will often differ from the store's actual strengths and weaknesses.) The marketing director and center manager should walk the center together and look at the stores as if seeing them for the first time, as consumers do. Ask yourself:

- Is the store unattractive?
- Is the service poor?
- Are the displays nonproductive?
- Is the entrance congested?
- Is the interior dirty?
- Are the signs attractive?

A visual audit may reveal the need for a retail consultant with visual merchandising expertise.

Does your research indicate that the center draws well but has a low ratio of converting traffic to sales? Look at the strength or weakness of sales volume in specific merchandise categories. Chart the annual sales per square foot in color-coded groups on a mall layout to focus on the strong and weak selling areas of the mall. This is extremely useful for placement of new stores or relocation of stores in the mall, as well as directing your attention to sales problems.

Does your center have a special situation? If the center is a new one, for example, you may want to bring in a retail consultant during the preopening process. If the center is being renovated and construction is in progress, a consultant can help motivate merchants to convert the inevitable traffic decline into compensatory sales. Other special situations include major competition and major events, such as the loss or gain of a large local employer. If a new center is opening nearby, one that will compete for your shoppers, a retail consultant can help improve selling techniques and the mall's image.

Once you have determined needs and defined goals, think about the specific results you want. A retail consultant to make successful stores more successful, or to help poorly performing stores upgrade their programs and improve sales? Improved selling techniques for managers and employees? Or, motivation and entertainment for store managers and owners? You may combine needs and goals, for example, by developing a year-long program focusing on sales and sales techniques that starts with a motivational seminar.

The next step is to find a consultant with the area of expertise, style, and focus that make that person a good match for your center. Many consulting firms attend ICSC functions and are available to discuss their programs. You can solicit specific information by:

- Obtaining a detailed outline of the program.
- Obtaining details on the materials presented and the manner of presentation.
- Talking to past clients of the consulting firm.
- Attending another program the consultant is giving in your area.
- Interviewing a consultant as you would a potential employee.
- Discussing with consultants the strengths and weaknesses of their programs.
- Determining how their program will meet your desired goals.

Echikson: Recommendations from others are good places to begin. It is advisable to seek out a multifaceted firm with broad expertise. Make sure the particular consultant assigned is familiar with your kind of center; if it's an outlet mall, for example, you would not want a high-fashion boutique specialist.

In general, specialty shop experience is more valuable than department store experience. The small stores in the center relate more easily to a consultant with specialty experience and are more likely to pay attention. In addition, specialty experience is generally broader and more entrepreneurial.

When place, time, and money have been settled and the only negotiating point left is references, ask for them. Consultants prefer to protect their references and will only allow a serious prospective client to call them.

ICSC: *How much should a consultant charge?*
Echikson: Good consultants are expensive—but you get what you pay for. You can expect to pay more than $1,000 a day for one-on-one consulting and approximately $5,000 for a center-wide seminar which can involve several consultants. If the owner has additional centers in the area, the seminar costs can be shared.

Consultants charge in one of three ways:

- By the day or hour.
- By the job or assignment.
- On a retainer basis, for time periods ranging from one month to a year.

Make sure you know exactly what you are getting for your money, including preparatory visits and follow-up.

ICSC: *Who should pay for the consultant?*
Echikson: For a centerwide seminar, the developer or owner usually pays. Occasionally the merchants association will fund the seminar. For one-on-one consultation with a group of retailers selected by the developer either for their potential or need, the developer ideally pays two-thirds and the retailers one-third of the cost. However, in real life the developer often pays the total cost and must expect in time—although there are no guarantees—to recoup the investment in overage rent or through the benefits of a stable retail population and improved general performance.
Aboussie: If a center has created a strong program with clearly defined goals, it should be possible to convince the developer that something in the best interest of the entire center is in the best interest of the owners. By supporting the

program, developers build necessary relationships with merchants and provide proof of their commitment to the center.

Another source of funds may be the merchants association budget or the marketing fund. However, these funds are typically limited and this kind of expenditure may have an adverse effect on advertising.

Store owners and the developer may also share the cost. Often, however, a local store manager cannot commit large amounts of money. The top amount is sometimes as little as $25, so if a fee is going to be charged it should not exceed what local stores can pay.

Another seminar-funding possibility is to open attendance to people outside your mall for a fee.

ICSC: *Who should attend a seminar given by a consultant?*
Aboussie: Review your original goals to determine your target audience—store managers and/or store employees? Then be sure to contact the local or regional store owner as well, so that the owner can encourage local personnel to attend. Never underestimate the influence that the owner or district or regional manager can have on the individual store manager's interest and enthusiasm.

If you decide to target only those retailers experiencing poor sales, pay special attention to your manner of presentation. Don't diminish enthusiasm by talking down to your audience, either during the invitation process or while the seminar is taking place.
Echikson: All retailers should be invited to the seminar, but some may not attend.

Anchors, or department stores, are often unlikely to come; if they do, they really cannot execute the consultants suggestions.

National chains will occasionally attend, especially if the invitation includes the regional or district manager. This not only prods the latter to encourage the local managers, it also has good public relations value. Remember, store managers are often allowed little flexibility over the variety of merchandise within their stores, and practically none from store to store. When, for example, a consultant suggests that the best way to take advantage of a center promotion is to consolidate all the clearance items from regional stores into a giant markdown area in the store in your center, the store manager may not be able to implement the idea. The regional manager, however, does have that authority. A regional manager who has either heard the consultant present the idea or been asked to hear it will be more likely to cooperate than one who has been excluded.

Regional chains, like those with four local shoe stores or three local furniture stores, often get the most out of a retail consultant. If the store is making money, the owner is probably pretty smart, and yet does not have the in-house resources of the larger chains. An alert owner will realize that even if the suggestions don't necessarily apply to the store in question, they may work for stores in other locations.

Locals, or mom-and-pop stores, will usually come to the seminar and benefit from it. If they have very little experience, there may be a problem as to the level at which the seminar should be given. That is why consultants with a wide breadth of experience and platform skills are a must.

Leasing agents should be considered, if they bring prospective tenants to the program. Seminars are a good selling point—they illustrate that the owners really care about the center.

Within each retail establishment, invite only the owner and/or manager. Invite all employees only if the consultant is giving a sales-training course and providing multilevel sessions.

ICSC: *How do you recruit and motivate retailers to attend?*
Aboussie: Recruiting retailers is one of the most challenging and important aspects of the program, for without good attendance, the program cannot be successful. Pay close attention to the overall timing of the program, as well as the timing of specific seminars and classes. If possible, offer a variety of times so stores can choose what's best for them.

At least six weeks before the event, the center manager and marketing director must set specific attendance goals. At that time, send out an attractive and exciting invitation to local and other managers. Ask the consultant if there are any national contacts which may be used to influence a local store manager to participate.

Follow up with weekly memos, newsletter articles, and information about the speaker and program to keep stores informed and motivated.

During the final three weeks, personal contact with each store, district, or regional manager is vital. Offer a special bonus or prize to the first merchants to sign up by an early deadline. Recruit dependable store managers as area captains to encourage participation. Or use your board of directors, advisory council, or other leaders to help boost attendance.

Echikson: The invitation should come from the developer/owner and should include a response card. If asked, the consultant will word the invitation for you.

Just prior to the seminar, after follow-up mailings and a personal visit to unresponsive stores, the consultant may arrive on site and walk the mall. This allows him to chat with the retailers, indirectly encouraging them to attend. It also educates the consultant on that particular center. Sometimes the consultant will invite the center manager and marketing director, or, at their suggestion, the center's most vocal or influential retailers to dinner. If you think this preseminar exposure would be useful to your center, make it part of the original agreement with the consultant.

ICSC: *What information about the particular center should a consultant have before arriving on site?*
Echikson: The consultant should be given information on:

- Basic area demographics—population, average family income, percent of dual-career families, cost of housing, growth trends, etc.
- Competing centers—their merchandise mix, strengths, and weaknesses.
- The tenant list, including store sales per square feet going back two or more years, plus general comments on each store's situation.

- Rents and lengths of leases for each tenant.
- Each retailer attending, to help the consultant customize the agenda.
- Key problems/opportunities affecting the center.

If the center cannot supply this information, the consultant should obtain it through research.

Using this information, the consultant develops an agenda which should be sent to center management and modified according to their suggestions. Any center hiring a consultant should insist on a program tailored to fit that particular center's needs.

Aboussie: The consultant should know your aims and goals, including which stores you want to focus on—a merchandise category, or stores in a particular wing or section of the mall. In addition to the information just mentioned, center management should be sure the consultant knows the following:

- Price point level for each store.
- Center layout, indicating the location of all stores.
- Analysis of stores' sales on a center map, color-coded to the sales performance of the stores.
- A list of specific stores on which the consultant should focus.

ICSC: *What type of follow-up should be done after the consultant leaves?*

Echikson: A letter signed by the developer or center manager and the consultant should be sent to seminar participants thanking them for their interest and encouraging them to call the consultant with any questions that have occurred to them.

The developer should also have given each participant an evaluation form—which could be prepared by the consultant—asking which parts of the seminar were most beneficial and which require more data, and so on.

In one-on-one consulting, the follow-up is different. When the consultation is over, the retailer should receive some specific agreed-upon action points on a "punch list." They might include:

- Elimination of hand-lettered signs.
- Taking specific return to vendor (RTV) or markdown action.
- Grouping merchandise clearance items together.
- Reevaluating the buying plan.
- Formation of an advertising cooperative with suppliers or complementary merchants.
- More aggressive participation in centerwide events.

In three to four weeks the consultant should call the merchant to see which items have been accomplished. Once an answer—which may overstate the improvements—has been provided, the consultant should confirm the results with center management.

In the ideal situation, the consultant makes a return visit. This is not always possible, but it is something that can be specified when the consulting agreement is signed. It is important for the consultant to develop a good working relationship with the center's management, marketing, and leasing professionals.

With a consultant on retainer there is the advantage of continual follow-up. The developer can call on the consultant whenever there is a problem, which gives merchants a sense of continuity.

Aboussie: Be sure that *prior* to leaving the session, each participant receives a comprehensive evaluation form. Center management should work with store managers to set up programs to continue the momentum created. There should also be a specific centerwide program, such as a year-long sales improvement competition, or monthly meetings held to reiterate specific skills or techniques. Try devoting a column in your monthly newsletter to the sales improvements made at specific stores.

ICSC: *When should the consultant come?*

Aboussie: Determine the best time to hold your seminar by referring to your goals. If you have a fairly standard situation—that is, no renovation or grand opening—and want to use consultant seminars as a method to improve your stores and increase sales, then hold the seminar just before a heavy selling season. For example, merchants realize that Christmas is a peak season and increase staff accordingly. These people should be not only available, but also qualified, educated, and enthusiastic. A consultant who could help bring this about might be most effective toward the end of October or early in November. Another important time might be before the spring or fall selling seasons.

Many marketing directors and center managers employ this type of seminar to introduce a new program at the annual meeting. Your retail consultant could be there to host seminars during the day and then be the guest speaker for the meeting.

Echikson: Help with merchandising is most useful in June or July when small stores are buying for Christmas. The best time to schedule a seminar is on two successive mornings, or, if feasible, on a Sunday. Occasionally two or three single-owner centers can be grouped together to increase the audience and spread the cost.

ICSC: *Where should centerwide meetings with a consultant take place?*

Echikson: In theory, the best learning environment is away from the center. However, this involves more time than most retailers can spare, so the best place realistically may be the center's community room. For a center without meeting facilities, a local bank, restaurant, or movie theater may provide free space.

Make sure the room is equipped for any audiovisual presentations the consultant may be making. Remember that your local electronics store will probably lend you a TV and a videocassette recorder.

Aboussie: Be sure the room you choose is clean, well lit, comfortable, heated or air-conditioned, private, easily accessible, and has a minimum of outside noise. Possible distractions should be considered when determining time and location. Remember, even food smells can be a distraction when using a private room in a restaurant or cafeteria.

ICSC: *How should the room be arranged?*

Aboussie: The consultant should give you a comprehensive list of equipment needed. It may include slide projectors, screens, videotape machines, flip charts, blackboards, film projectors, felt-tip pens, chalk, microphones, public-address systems, and cassette tapes. When renting equipment, try to have an operator on site the entire time, as well as backup equipment available immediately. It is disastrous to go to all the trouble and expense of hiring a consultant and getting retailers to attend and then lose hours due to faulty equipment.

Echikson: Arrange the room as informally as possible. Try for table seating rather than classroom-like rows of chairs. Serve refreshments. Make sure each participant has a name tag giving name and store affiliation.

ICSC: *What results can a center expect from a consultant?*

Echikson: From one visit, the center should get positive feelings about the owner from retailers and some level of improved store results. The degree of cooperation between merchants and center management should also improve. Quarterly or semiannual visits can lead to more concrete achievements. The price per session goes down after the initial session because there is less homework for the consultant to do.

It is important to select a retail consulting firm which has specialists in various disciplines so that programs can effectively target specific needs.

Merchandising is a key element in retailing and the one where many local merchants are weakest and can gain the most from a consultant. They may learn more about inventory planning and control, open-to-buy calculations, markdown implementation, vendor relationships, and terms.

Marketing is another area where the smaller stores are weak. They often rely on the center to do their job for them. A good consultant can help a retailer learn who its customers are and how best to reach them, paving the way for stocking what those customers want to buy.

Sales training is an area where even the big chains may falter. A sales training program with follow-up can benefit every store in the center.

A developer should expect a consultant to improve the bottom line. However, it will not happen overnight, and it will not happen to the same degree in every store.

Aboussie: Individual merchants as well as entire centers benefit from the specialized training retail consultants provide. However, you must remember that bringing in a consultant is only the beginning of a powerful, ongoing program designed to help retailers improve sales. As you decide on the best consultant for your center, begin motivating and recruiting retailers to attend, and go on to evaluate and stimulate follow-up of the program, you will be setting in motion a process of interaction with, and concern for, your retailers that should become an integral part of the overall success of the center.

Karen Aboussie, CMD, is assistant vice president and director of corporate marketing for Goodman Segar Hogan, Inc., a commercial real estate company in Virginia which manages 15,615,000 square feet of shopping space ranging from strip centers to super regionals. Ms. Aboussie is a member of the International Council of Shopping Centers' Certified Marketing Director Committee and speaks frequently at ICSC marketing conferences.

Richard Echikson is chairman of Retail Consultants, Inc. in Millburn, New Jersey, which provides consulting services to guide center owners. Mr. Echikson has been a speaker at International Council of Shopping Centers' conferences and Idea Exchanges, and is a faculty member of the International Council of Shopping Centers' University of Shopping Centers, where he conducts a course entitled "Helping Merchants Help Themselves."

3
Using Visual Merchandising to Improve Sales

• **Joseph Weishar**, New Vision Studios, Inc.

Visual merchandising creates the impression customers receive in the store. In-store presentation is responsible for more sales than all other media combined. Consumers express their perception of merchandise desirability in one measurable way: They buy or they don't buy. They don't verbalize their perceptions, because as consumers, they don't know the language of retail aesthetics. If we want to visually communicate with the person who makes a purchase we must understand why and how a perception is formed.

Consumer behavior in a retail environment can be anticipated to a greater degree than previously thought. Their responses to physical and psychological stimuli may be codified and evaluated to provide the whys and hows of consumer behavior.

Consumers form an image of the store from several or all of the following when entering a retail space:

- Merchandise quantity and style.
- Quality and clarity of presentation.
- Architecture.
- Floor layout: aisles, fixtures, traffic patterns.
- Lighting.
- Color.
- Signs: wording and design.

All the senses go into perceiving, and perception is the customer's reality—the environment of a store. Sight, smell, hearing, and touch tell customers whether they are in a designer boutique or an off-price toy store. Sight, however, is the most important. What follows are some rules of thumb you and your retailers should know about visual merchandising.

INVENTORY

Full Shelves Inspire Shoppers' Faith
Customers have an intuitive mechanism which, though unspoken, balances stock levels and total space against price and quality. If a store meets a customer's expectations, it has credibility.

Two major rules of retailing relate to inventory:

1. Give the customers what they came to buy.
2. If you're out of stock on basics, you're out of business.

Since most customers are shopping for basics, a good merchant will be well supplied with them. Basic merchandise is usable at least nine months a year and must be replaced due to use or style change (for example, shoes). Basics can be accessories, such as women's pantyhose, or classics, such as a man's navy-blue blazer. These are items a merchant must always keep in stock, in a full range of sizes and in popular colors. As you walk about the center, you may be able to help retailers by noticing whether their inventory in basics seems adequate. Use your intuition backed by the following information on some categories' basics, which include:

- Linens—solid-color towels and sheets.
- Men's clothing—shirts, socks, underwear.
- Women's clothing—blouses.
- Sewing supplies—thread, patterns.
- Lingerie—brassieres and underpants.
- Accessories—ties, handbags, shoes, hosiery, jewelry, cosmetics.

Despite cultural differences in each market, every category of merchandise has a key item. That key item is generally an *expendable basic* and the most frequently purchased in a category. Make your own list and then compare it with your store's sales figures—most of the time your intuition will be right.

An illustration of how well intuition can correlate with actual sales appeared in "Yuppies *Do* Have Feelings, Says Pier 1 Study," in *Chain Store Age Executive,* May 1988. In the article, John Mathewson, market research manager of Pier 1 Imports, a specialty home furnishings retailer, commented on the results of a special research project. He said, "the study gave us more detail and reassurance that what we suspected in our guts [was] true." The study's results improved, instead of changing, the focus of Pier 1's marketing strategy. Continuing, the article said, "the study revealed that college-educated shoppers turn to specialty stores for ideas of how to improve their home. From this the store has learned that one way of servicing the customer is to improve displays."

One good retailing trick is to present basics so that they appear exciting. They must not be buried under jazzy presentations for more trendy merchandise. Basics should be placed to be seen by the customer upon entry. This gives the shopper the secure feeling that the basics will be in stock after a tour of the store.

Product Market Dominance—Increasing Market Share

In addition to being strong in basics, a merchant must aim to be dominant in one merchandise area within the store's category. A men's store might dominate in Oxford button-downs, or a cosmetics store in lipsticks. The store should stand out in the customer's mind as *the* place to shop for a particular item, preferably a basic item that must be renewed or replaced several times a year. The perception of an in-stock, broad assortment is what the customer remembers most about the store. The market dominance this gives a merchant helps build sales.

To give an example: a specialty store selling women's undergarments and loungewear might consider adding robes and sleepwear to its inventory from a national manufacturer's line. But this merchandise would take up a large amount of space and the specialty store would still have a smaller selection of robes and sleepwear than the mall anchor store, leading customers to choose the department store for this merchandise. The small store's sales and profits would probably improve if it did not stock the robes and sleepwear—except at Christmas—and concentrated instead on high-volume, high-profit items like bras and panties. They take up less room and could allow the store to dominate in that merchandise group in the center.

A merchant should make the choice of market dominance based on:

1. Past success with particular merchandise. Merchants can learn to track the success of particular items by studying cash register receipts for the number of transactions of these units, as well as noting items they have a special feel for.
2. Media information as to what is selling and what might sell well in the future.
3. Influences on product-buying decisions, especially entertainment media. A merchant might want to give salespeople notepads and ask them to list trend-setting items they notice or note customer requests for items not in stock.

Some examples of past media influences and the consumer products they affected are:

Out of Africa	Khaki
Wild Ones	Leather jackets, motorcycles
Rebel Without a Cause	Jeans, T-shirts
Karate Kid	Training parlors
On Golden Pond	Jane Fonda aerobics
Breaking Away	Bicycling
Marathon Man	Athletic equipment
E.T.	Related dolls
Miami Vice	Men's pastel leisurewear

There is also a symbiotic relationship between the movie/movies playing in the mall theater and the type of merchandise sold in the shops.

4. Advice from center management—who know the total pic-

ture better than any single retailer—about holes in the center's merchandise offerings and how they might be filled. A developer can get this information by comparing sales from one center to another.

Saying that inventory must be adequate does not mean it must be overwhelmingly large. Too much stock of a single item tells customers to wait for the next markdown.

The quantity should be in proportion to:

- Store traffic—the number of customers on the sales floor.
- The ability to replace items quickly.
- The amount of service being offered.

A store that provides a great deal of service can have a small amount of inventory showing, while a self-service store must have large or bulk merchandise presentation. The goal is to have enough items to hold the full range of sizes until replacement with new merchandise or recoordination with other offerings is possible.

MERCHANDISE DISPLAY

Every store or department has three zones from the principal entrance: *the front line* or main aisle presentation; *the department center*, for bulk or classification grouping; and *the wall*, or perimeter area, which serves as a focal point.

The Front Line

The nearest exposition of merchandise for sale is the front line. It should not be the lease line because customers tend to walk past the first presentation if it is too close to the point of entry. Just consider the mall center court to be a street. Some shops use the sidewalk while department stores have a foyer and a set-back to the first counter. In malls many stores do not allow for this attitudinal adjustment space. Merchants must devote a certain percentage of their square footage to allow the customer to enter and feel comfortable before being challenged to make a buying decision. In a deep store, say 100 feet deep by 25 feet of frontage, six feet at the front for penetration is not too much.

Since this is a difficult zone to control, the center can help merchants make their front space productive by spotlighting the front of the store from common area positions.

Presentations from the entry to the back wall should entice the customer, by increments, to penetrate further into the store. The front line should:

1. Contain the shop's feature presentations—mannequin or merchandise displays based on seasonal, monthly, or special promotional themes or new selections.
2. Have a visual appeal which draws the eye forward or creates some kind of pattern that gets the customer's attention, such as presentations at different heights.
3. Contain fixtures—devices that hold merchandise for sale— turned so that the front side is angled 45° off the main traffic entry aisle, instead of facing it head-on. This layout induces penetration because it is easier for the body to turn 45° rather than 90°.
4. Change every *two weeks* in keeping with the store's promotional calendar and the need to get the attention of loyal customers, who tend to shop with that frequency.
5. Contain any item that has been advertised.

There is an exception to this rule, however, with advertised sale merchandise. In a storewide clearance, where one-third of the merchandise is probably being marked down, these items should not monopolize the front line. It should not look as if everything in the store is marked down when there is new merchandise on hand as well. Some sale merchandise can be in the front line with the remainder bulked directly behind it in a concentrated arrangement. Place the racks to draw the consumer into the department, not to "cherry-pick" your front line.

Feature presentations will be effective if merchants:

• Remember that "less is more": each feature presentation should tell only one story.

- Combine merchandise that is traditionally "hot" with merchandise that is *seasonally* hot. Use the traditionally hot item of women's blouses, for example, to feature metallic and sequined tops during the Christmas holiday season, brightly colored blouses in the summer, pastels in the spring, and jewel tones in the fall. These items are called "fashion basics."
- Make use of the intense focus that diagonals get by highlighting merchandise at the top of pyramids. A diagonal is more eye-catching, since our eyes automatically perceive vertical and horizontal lines. Diagonals also evoke sharper emotional reactions, such as falling, leaning, triangulation, perspective convergence, movement, and speed. Be judicious, however, in your use of any one eye-catcher: Overuse is misuse. Too many triangles can be as boring as too many face outs or too much shoulder hang.

The Department Center

The department center, or main merchandise presentation area, should have:

1. Short, diagonal aisles.
2. Depth in backup merchandise for the feature presentations. The buying team must be made aware of this goal.
3. Highly visible basics. They need not be in the direct line of sight, but should be near an entry pattern of the store or department.
4. A clear showing by fixture presentation, or with assists by display, of the second, third, or fourth themes in each category area. More than one merchandise story is told at any time during the yearly cycle. The center area (if the store or department is deep enough to have more than one line of merchandise before the wall) is also available for some display presentation which will further assist customers to see the key groups within a category.
5. Merchandise that is changed every three months for a seasonal freshening.
6. A new look every six months. Old stock should be cleared and replaced with new merchandise.

The Wall: A Merchandising Focal Point

The wall should display merchandise related to feature presentations. After customers have looked at the feature, their eyes should be drawn back to the wall, where merchandise related to the feature is displayed in a full assortment. These wall displays are known as "focal points." They are what draw customers into a department or store and encourage them to make purchases.

Some virtues of a wall are that it can:

- Increase the customer traffic throughout the store, because getting the customer to the department perimeter increases the distance traveled within the store. Distance traveled relates more directly to sales per entering shopper per square foot of selling space than any other measurable consumer variable.
- Hold large amounts of merchandise.
- Be used for shelving and/or hanging.
- Be the merchandise sign for a given period, changing the fashion story for a whole department or store.
- Tell a multiple fashion story in a single space.
- Make customers focus on particular items or names, seeing what merchants want them to see.
- Sell more high-margin merchandise—on which the difference between cost to merchant and retail price is higher than average—than a floor fixture. The wall is obviously not the place for sale items.

Good examples of profitable wall displays for larger stores are:

- Men's socks—formal and athletic, five to six high on the wall.
- Women's packaged hosiery—8 to 12 tiers on the wall with a leg display above.
- Brassieres—packaged (all sizes) or open (smaller sizes).
- Briefs—vertical by color, horizontal by size; large sizes folded on lower shelves or side-hung.
- Accessories—all, including costume jewelry. Handbags on shelves always look and sell better than handbags hung on

floor units with underslung J-hooks. Hanging bags on this type of holder shows more of the strap than the face of the bag.
- Housewares—small packaged items rather than large box units. Walls can hold more than shelves and the multiple effect strengthens the presentation.

A small store should use its walls for a continuous display of its full line, plus seasonally adjusted merchandise which should change frequently. The seasonal merchandise should be on the area of the wall that is seen first by entering customers.

Merchandisers generally like to have more than one display on the wall, but have difficulty creating breaks in the pattern of presentation. The wall needs to be composed of positive (merchandise) and negative (wall) space to create a flowing image on a surface that by its very nature affords no architectural breaks.

Columns: A Mid-floor Bonanza

Columns are generally overlooked as potential merchandise display space during the store's layout planning process. Instead they are thought of as:

1. Ceiling supports.
2. Main aisle markers.
3. Mirror holders.
4. Nuisances, to be hidden in wall divider store partitions.

There are some very smart merchandisers, however, who are positioning merchandise around a column and even extending the column with wing walls. A column may easily provide an additional twelve feet of wall space. The amount of merchandise exposed in relation to the square and cubic footage gives the consumer an idea of price. Shops that cater to the upper market can also use columns to emphasize quality merchandise and heighten the sense of exclusivity.

The use of columns for merchandise is a concern for loss prevention personnel because they block a clerk's view from the cash/wrap counter. This may be a legitimate concern, but so far I have found that inventory loss can be prevented if more shoppers are present and if there is a motivated staff circulating within the store.

BROKEN SIZES

The Art of Fast-Moving Fashion

Merchants must have a system that alerts them to stock movement and lets them know when there are holes in the assortment. Even in the best-stocked store there will be outages, of course, but the goal should be to continue to project an image of completeness for each display. There are several ways to do this, which include:

- Shifting or removing fixtures when the quantity of stock and styles is not sufficient to fill the fixture. Putting unused fixtures in temporary storage is the direct responsibility of a well-trained staff.
- Recoordinating garments with others of similar style, color, or price. Once sizes are broken for featured items that have been selling well, the merchandise should be moved into the department center or, for a smaller store, to the wall where most merchandise is presented, and grouped into end-use categories. For example, a blouse that had been part of a coordinated outfit could be placed with similar merchandise by type—sporty or dressy—and then by color. At the end of three to six months, this merchandise should be marked down. Markdown items should be arranged by size first and then by color within size.

Featured items that have not been selling well should be moved from a prime location to a secondary location, as above. If they still do not sell, they should be recoordinated as a group and marked down quickly on a special markdown rack.

Old merchandise makes new merchandise look old. When a sell down or style "check-out" happens faster than expected, there are several methods to cover these visual holes:

- Use more mannequins. Each mannequin takes up the space of one fixture (60-100 garments).
- Use photographs, posters, or wall displays. Every four feet of wall space equals 40-100 garments or, if it contains a display, no merchandise.
- Establish wide secondary aisles, from 4 to 6 feet wide.
- Use four-armed fixtures, which hold forty fewer garments, instead of circular ones.

Broken-size merchandising is a way of life for any store in a fast-moving fashion business. In order to appear to, or actually, change the presentation, the key area of a department should be re-dressed once a week, or at least in keeping with the number of visits from your most loyal shopper.

Some progressive merchandisers actually design entire collections that can be coordinated and recoordinated when one item of the collection outsells the rest.

SIGNS

There are a few basic rules about signs:

1. Use as few as possible. It is more effective to speak with merchandise than with signs.
2. Word them carefully, using adjectives and adverbs sparingly. Certain key words attract shoppers: *you, money, save, new, easy, love, discover, results, health, proven, free, guarantee.* Don't overuse them on one sign.
3. Be timely. Special-event signs should change when the event does.
4. Make sure the sign reflects the store. Small signs—and small entrances—suggest exclusiveness; large signs—and large entrances—communicate the message of a price-conscious retailer that offers basic stock and nonexclusive fashions.
5. Use exact price information instead of percentage discounts; it is easier to understand. Customers are also attracted by

price reductions such as "two for one" or "three for two" or "buy two get one free."

6. Don't submerge the store's identity under a barrage of signs from manufacturers; that is, don't become a warehouse for brands. Although some manufacturers supply excellent point-of-purchase fixtures and display units, the fact that they are free does not necessarily make them the right choice for a particular store, especially one with a fashion image.

   If a manufacturer or designer-styled fixture is used, have the manufacturer explain the proper use of the fixture, including the merchandise levels and delivery cycles necessary to keep the level of stock in the presentation creditable.

   No matter what line of merchandise is to be shown, it is the sole responsibility of the store management to accept only those fixtures that fit within the stated image of the store, including stock levels per sales hour ratios. For example, one store grouped different nationally owned labels in one department, but dictated size and color specifications for the designer logo on their signs.

7. Strike the right balance between the number of signs—their size, color, type, and style—and the price/quality/service image of the store. Lack of signs, combined with merchandise in a very casual arrangement, may indicate generous service, while an abundance of signs reinforces a self-service operation.

8. Make sure signs are readable. The most legible combination is black type on a yellow background; however, this combination also conveys the impression of low-priced merchandise. In general, white or light printing against a dark background is more readable than dark on white.

LIGHTING—FOR COST-EFFECTIVE GLAMOUR

Used well, lighting is one of the retailer's most flexible, powerful tools. Fluorescent, high-intensity, nondirectional light means lower price, as in supermarkets or volume-oriented discounters, whereas incandescent lighting says fashion and a certain exclusiveness.

Most fashion stores have a few key areas where the product and/or the customer require the best possible lighting. These are:

1. The checkout counter.
2. Floor mirrors.
3. Dressing rooms.

A daylight fluorescent light above a mirror, for example, can distort your skin color, shadow your eyes, and change the color of the merchandise, with totally uncomplimentary results. In this instance, I prefer the use of either frosted lamps or sconces on each side of the mirror and on the same plane as the face in conjunction with a back light for a halo effect around the head. The result is a customer who looks better, feels better and, therefore—hopefully—buys more.

Supermarkets are using highly sophisticated methods of lighting that make meat look redder, produce more appealing, frozen foods bluer, and so on.

Every store needs focusable lights. All the manager has to know is the difference between a spotlight and a floodlight to highlight an object properly.

One reason to avoid cool or daylight fluorescent lighting is that it—along with cool colors on the walls and ceiling—casts a light that is too blue-green, a shade associated with hospitals and institutions. Traditional fluorescent lighting also flickers, making the ambiance less desirable. However, new fluorescents have already been developed which give the same color range as incandescents.

COLOR

People prefer the primary and secondary colors—deep shades of red, blue, yellow, green, orange, and violet. Intense color also goes with seasonal merchandise, or merchandise that is being featured. Primary color backgrounds can indicate

---

CASE STUDY: EFFECTIVE VISUAL MERCHANDISING COMES TO A RETAILER

About three years ago a chain of discount stores selling housewares, linens, toys, and clothing had a cost-cutting program that had gone so far that profits and volume were declining. In order to reverse this process, the chain took a new approach to merchandising, much of it based on the principles of visual merchandising. Result: a sales increase of 25% in the pilot store in the first year.

The steps they took:

1. Improved wall presentations. Walls are now no farther than 30 feet from any aisle—the maximum distance for visual impact—and merchandise is displayed on the walls in focal points that relate to feature presentations.

2. Changed aisles from straight runs off a racetrack plan to diagonals, with no merchandise in any department more than 30 feet from a customer in any aisle. Instead of reducing available floor space, this layout gives a more open feeling and enhances presentation of goods for maximum visibility and increased turnover. It makes the store look more like a department store and less like a discounter.

3. Made the space more inviting by painting the high ceiling a dark color to lower it, perceptually, to a more human

---

one of three things:

1. A seasonal promotion.
2. A hot-selling item area.
3. A walk-through zone.

Stores that sell basics should have a background of neutral colors—greys and tans. Black and white are not neutrals and should be treated as carefully as primary colors. Neutrals are also right for departments simulating living situations, such as those selling home furnishings. People also prefer earth tones, such as those ranging from warm greys to scale, then animated it by installing "space frames"—white metal grids that give a high-tech look.

4. Re-did the lighting, using spotlights attached to the ceiling grids close to the merchandise in combination with existing fluorescents. This creates the impression of a giant boutique.

5. Started using columns instead of hanging signs for merchandise presentation and identification. This raises merchandise-level expectations.

6. Eliminated most interior walls, using metal grids instead to create occasional eye-stoppers throughout the store. These grids never interfere with visibility through the diagonal aisles to the well-merchandised back walls.

7. Drastically reduced the number of items carried in hard lines, such as toys or housewares, since competition in these areas with super specialty stores was impossible. Instead it was decided to carry only the best-sellers, aiming for high volume with very steep discounts, and using them as traffic builders for more profitable soft goods, such as household linens and wearables.

8. Replaced shelving with "stack-em-high" platforms for hard lines. Instead of 12 on a shelf, 12 dozen items are displayed on a freestanding platform, or on a "skid" that has come directly from the shipping truck to the floor, thus reducing stocking time and labor costs.

9. *Gave all staff the responsibility and authority for change and maintenance of the new layout.*

deep burgundies, including flesh colors but excluding pinks, and will stay longer in areas decorated with these shades than they will in more vibrantly decorated areas.

APPROACHING THE RETAILER

Becoming educated about visual merchandising puts center management in a position to give advice on the subject to retailers. But there is no guarantee that they will listen. Retailers, like others, are naturally wary of unsolicited advice, especially when it comes from someone outside their field, and particularly when it comes from the landlord.

To convince the retailers in your center of your sincerity, you might consider helping out, say, at Christmas, with selling or stocking or working with the store's display person. Another way to gain credibility is to approach the merchant indirectly. Talk about a known mutual interest first, something that is not threatening to the merchant, and then become more specific about visual merchandising. Once the merchant is listening, break things down into basic terms. Be specific about what is wrong and give suggestions about how to fix it, making examples of other stores in the center who have tried the same or similar strategies successfully. Retailers know that their competition is not store-to-store within the mall but rather mall-to-mall, and should welcome these suggestions.

Change is the heart of retailing. By noticing when things are beginning to look stale and making some tactful suggestions for improved visual merchandising, the center manager can help individual merchants improve their sales, as well as those of the shopping center.

Joseph Weishar, president and founder of New Vision Studios, Inc. in New York City is a store and shop design and construction consultant. For the past 12 years, he has applied his background in fine art, graphics, theater, and merchandising to codify merchandise presentation techniques to facilitate the training of all staff levels in a retail store. He has spoken at International Council of Shopping Centers' conferences and he writes a regular column on visual merchandising for *Visual Merchandising and Store Design* magazine.

4

Helping Retailers Use Research Information

• Robert M. Jones, CMD, Stillerman Jones & Company, Inc.

As retailers make choices among different possibilities in merchandising, presenting, advertising, and promoting goods for sale, the information that can help them falls into five categories:

1. Results of shopper surveys, typically done as exit interviews in the center.
2. Results of telephone surveys in the center's market area.
3. Information from focus groups of 8 to 12 people representing either a segment or a cross section of shoppers, who are interviewed in depth by a trained moderator.
4. Demographics or the study of the characteristics of the people—such as age and family income—who live in a market area.
5. Miscellaneous market information.

SHOPPER SURVEYS

In a shopper survey, 300 to 500 people are questioned as they are leaving a center. Their answers to the questions give a "snapshot" of how the center looks at a particular moment and indicate the shopping orientation of the center's frequent customers. (Although the survey will also pick up infrequent shoppers, most respondents will be frequent ones.) Naturally, a shopper survey can only give information on people who are already center patrons. Typical questions include:

1. What is your primary purpose in being at the center? Did you come with a particular purchase or specific store in mind or were your goals less focused?
2. Where did you come from—home, work, another center?
3. Where are you going after you leave the center?
4. How did you get to the center—car, bus, or other means?
5. How much time did you spend at the center?
6. What stores did you visit?
7. Where did you make any purchases?
8. What is the total dollar amount of your purchases?
9. What are your suggestions for improving the center? Additional stores, services, ambiance, other?
10. How would you grade this center in relation to other centers in the area?
11. How frequently do you visit this center? Other centers?
12. What kind of media do you prefer—radio, TV stations, newspapers?

Questions of a personal nature, yielding demographic information, might be asked late in the interview.

A shopper survey provides useful information for retailers because it deals with the immediate shopping experience, and certain facts about specific stores may emerge. Although it is not typical for the survey questions to pinpoint certain retailers, respondents will frequently mention a store where their experience was noteworthy—either good or bad. The answers to the sixth, seventh, and ninth questions are important in this regard.

TELEPHONE SURVEYS

A telephone survey yields information about people in the center's market area which, as defined by a market survey, is roughly the same as the center's "trade area." Here the relevant population, or "universe," is the whole area. In a telephone survey, questioners can derive wider data about competitive patronage and the center's nonshoppers than in a shopper survey. Since the respondents are people who are typically home during the day, however, a telephone survey may not be good for gathering demographic data for broad social and economic generalizations about a population.

Frequently asked questions in a telephone survey include:

• How often do you shop at each of the centers in the area?
• Which center do you prefer, and why?
• What factors would cause you to prefer our center?

The last question is aimed at getting at real obstacles, such as a parking problem, as opposed to nonspecific complaints.

Although it is easy to see how answers to these general questions could yield specific information about retailers, they generally find information from shopper surveys more useful than that gleaned from telephone surveys.

FOCUS GROUPS

A focus group yields subjective or qualitative, as opposed to numerical, information. Usually focus groups are held in groups of three (one at a time), each with eight to twelve participants who may represent either a segment or a cross section of shoppers. The trained moderator of a focus group can probe for perceptions, attitudes, and habits of shoppers, looking for the reasons behind the percentages of yes and no answers. Each focus group is not a sufficient sample of the market to make statistical generalizations. When interpreters start hearing the same thing in several groups, however, they may conclude that the feeling is widely held.

Focus groups are an inexpensive way to test reactions to advertising, either print or electronic. They are also good for discovering the unknown. As an example, a focus group might reveal that people perceive that a center's renovation made prices higher even if such is not the case. No one at the center might have foreseen that this perception might arise. As the focus group has brought out, it is now a real problem with which the center must deal.

A focus group may also highlight situations that center people take for granted, and which consumers may not. For example, there might be an odor emanating from food, planters, fountains, or varnish that consumers find objectionable.

DEMOGRAPHICS

Traditionally, demographic information was census information—broad social and economic data—and surveys aimed at discovering the spending potential of the people living in a market area. This basic information included:

1. Age distribution.
2. Income distribution.
3. Racial distribution.
4. Total population of the area.
5. Total number of households in the area.
6. Average household size.

Now, however, some demographic researchers go beyond household income information and analyze information about education, occupation, marital status, number and ages of children in the household, whether the wife works, and more. Researchers then statistically group people into 44 to 48 lifestyle categories and give them fanciful names such as "Leave It to Beaver" and "Palm Trees and Condos."

Beyond these lifestyle groupings is psychographic profiling, which further segments demographic groups according to personality, benefits sought, user status (first-time user, nonuser, etc.), usage rate, loyalty, sensitivity to quality, price, service, and the like.

MISCELLANEOUS MARKET INFORMATION

Other information helpful to retailers might include:

1. Paydays of major employers in the market.

2. Ratings of different media.
3. Average time and depth of snowfall.
4. Center sales standards—per square foot—for particular categories of retailers, such as shoes or gifts.
5. Industry sales standards.
6. Comparisons of how a particular chain is doing in several different centers.

PRESENTING THE INFORMATION

Center management cannot simply turn over all of this information to retailers and expect them to make sense of it. It must be analyzed and edited carefully, then presented to a decision maker, usually the store's owner or a regional manager. The presentation can be a mini research report or a live presentation, but in any case the retailer must leave with something that is written down and not more than a few pages long. Also, the retailer must be approached with the conclusions for that business already drawn. Rather than play guessing games about what the retailer might be able to conclude from uninterpreted data, center management must understand something about the retailer's business before the conversation begins.

Analysis basically examines each of the bodies of data and compares them to one another. Some examples are:

1. Comparing the quality of your center's shoppers with the quality of the market on a particular factor, such as age distribution. This commonly used measure is known as the "relative draw index" or the "penetration index." It tells you where your strengths and weaknesses are. If the market contains 10% teenagers aged 13-18 and 15% of your shoppers are in that range, you are drawing one-and-a-half times what you might expect relative to the market. That tells a retailer that this is a teenage-oriented center, and may suggest that it should merchandise for teenagers. Or, the information may indicate that the center is already merchandised to teens and needs to appeal to an older group.

2. Comparing the percent of traffic with the percent of sales for different groups, such as age, sex, income, or race. This gives the "sales contribution." It lets you know who are the heavy, and who the light, spenders. From this information a retailer may conclude that the light spenders do not offer much potential. Or you may compare your center's expenditure patterns to some industry standards and conclude that there is more potential spending there than you are achieving, which means some changes are needed.

3. Comparing a shopper survey with demographics and industry bench marks.

4. Studying "shopper conversions," that is, what percent of shoppers are converted to buyers—the result of comparing the answers to "Where did you go?" with those to "Where did you buy?" Theoretically, this comparison should yield information for every store in the center. In reality, a typical shopper visits fewer than four stores, so the percentage who go into any one store may be too small a sample to yield statistically significant information. Still, putting several stores together can yield information about a category and can suggest why certain stores have problems.

5. Studying people's replies when asked what stores or items they would like in the center. If those stores, or stores selling those items, are already present, you know immediately that they are not doing a good job of letting people know they are there, or else they are not succeeding in serving the needs of potential customers. If the question turns up interest in merchandise or food that is truly not available in the center, that may suggest either bringing in a new retailer or asking an existing one to start carrying additional items.

WHAT RETAILERS NEED TO KNOW

In addition to the information described above, the typical retailer should know:

1. The geographic and basic demographic dimensions of the center's market area.

2. The strengths and weaknesses of the traffic draw, and what this means to the retailer.
3. The shopping pattern of typical shoppers—where they are coming from and going to, where they shopped, where they bought, and how much they spent.
4. What stores draw traffic for their particular store, and from which other stores the traffic is drawn.
5. How the store is doing in its category.
6. The marketing team's strategies for the center—how the market is expected to change over time, and how the marketing strategy is expected to change the market.

The answers to the fourth item above may suggest the possibility of holding promotions for mutual benefit. The

---

THREE MINICASES

1. A jewelry store in suburban Virginia was advertising in a Washington newspaper. Research showed that the paper did not have good penetration into the trade area. This research was used to convince the district manager to spend more dollars on local advertising to better penetrate the trade area.

2. A women's specialty store in a specialty shopping area was having problems. Research showed that:
• The store was not attracting its share of center traffic.
• Conversion of traffic to sales was relatively low.

This information was shared with the store, which made the folowing improvements:
• The storefront presentation was changed.
• Inside, visual merchandising was improved.
• An awning was added to make the store more visible.

Sales improved significantly.

3. Research showed that an apparel store had relatively low shopper conversion. The center manager was concerned about low merchandise levels in the store, fearing they were hindering sales performance.

The research that supported that suspicion was shared with the store manager and steps were taken to increase inventory levels. Sales performance improved.

---

answer to the fifth item will help retailers decide where to spend their time—they may want to limit it to stores that are doing well. The last item above may help the retailers adjust their advertising or promotional strategies.

Sharing pertinent information with your retailers will not only instill confidence in the job center management is doing but will also help the retailers modify their merchandise display and selling techniques to improve retail productivity.

Robert M. Jones, CMD, is a principal in Stillerman Jones & Company, Inc., of Indianapolis, Indiana, an international shopping center and retail services firm which specializes in marketing research and leasing. Mr. Jones is a frequent instructor at International Council of Shopping Centers' Institutes and has served on the Admissions and Governing Committee for the Certified Marketing Director professional designation.

5

Increasing Revenue With Financial Basics

• **John C. Williams,** John C. Williams Consultants Ltd.

The management of money is one of the most important factors in a store's success. Understanding what's behind the financial formulas and numbers used in retailing is essential if center management is to help its merchants and the shopping center increase revenue.

Basically, retailers make a profit the same way most other businesses do. They generate revenue and create sufficient margins from which to pay expenses and have funds for a profit. It sounds simple, but running a store is a uniquely complex business that involves keeping many things going smoothly at one time. These elements of retailing include:

- A wide diversity of shoppers.
- Staff.
- Inventory assortments and levels.
- Buying.
- The physical environment.
- Advertising.
- Sales promotion.
- Support services.
- Administration.
- Materials handling.

- Banking.
- Vendor relationships.
- Finances.

It is important to remember the multitude of factors and pressures that affect store management and owners when working with them. By accommodating their needs with regard to time and resources you can help them with their prime function—serving customers.

DIFFERENT PATHS TO PROFIT

There are two distinct paths or formulas for generating retail profit, measured both as a percent of sales and as return on investment (ROI). Successful stores tend to clearly follow one of the two paths. There is the high-road store, which has a distinctly high gross margin, costs, investment, quality of service, and environment. Then there is the low-road store, which operates on a distinctly lower gross margin, costs,

SUCCESSFUL RETAILER TYPES			
	Store A	Store B	Store C
Sales	100%	100%	100%
Cost of goods	45–50%	70–80%	30–35%
Gross margin	45%	30%	65–70%
Expenses			
Wages	20%	15%	20–30%
Advertising, sales promotion, etc.	5%	2%	5%
Occupancy, etc.	10%	6%	15%
Banking & miscellaneous	5%	5%	5%
Total expenses	40%	28%	50%
Profit (% of sales)	5%	2%	15%
Inventory turnover	3–5%	6–15%	20–40%

investment, and service levels. It should be noted that the low margin/low investment stores often generate a greater ROI than the high-road stores.

There is also a third type of store, typical of fast-food operations, with high gross margin, wages, and net profit, as well as fairly intensive capital costs per square foot.

In the table above, store "A" is an apparel store characterized by a high gross margin, fair to low stock turnover, and high investment costs in decor, fixtures, and accounts receivable. Store "B" is a food store with the opposite characteristics, that is, a low gross margin, high stock turnover, and low investment costs in decor, fixtures, and accounts receivable. Store "C," a fast-food pizza shop, ranks high in capital cost and very high in gross margin and turnover.

Profit-path clues to look for may include any one of the following:

- Is the store clearly presenting dollar-saving value?
- Is the store clearly presenting an emotional, high-service experience?
- Is the store giving shoppers mixed messages as to level of service and value?

UNDERSTANDING STORE OPERATIONS

Once again numbers reveal the truth about retail operations. Areas for examination are sales, cost of goods, markups, gross margin, and expenses.

Sales are always referred to in net terms, that is, after sales tax and refunds. All retail financial figures are discussed as a percent of net (100%) sales. The bottom line is simple—no matter how wonderful or awful a store is, its real success is reflected in the shoppers' eyes and measured by how they vote at the cash register.

Cost of goods sold (COGS) is literally the cost of the merchandise. It may vary as a percent of sales as follows:

- 80% —for discounted electronics.
- 70% —for appliances or some fast-food outlets.

- 60% —for children's-wear basics; books; millinery.
- 50% —"keystone"—most stores in the mall.
- 45% —for fashion apparel.

Big chains can affect the COGS by 10% with direct, volume buying. Independents and small chains cannot significantly influence merchandise costs.

Markup, or marking, or mark-on, are the terms retailers use to describe the dollar amount they add on to the cost of merchandise, in terms of a percent of retail; a 50% markup is 50% of the selling price or 100% of the cost price. Thus if the retail price of a man's suit is $300 and the COGS is $150, the markup will be $150, or 50%. A book priced at $25 with a COGS of $15 has a markup of $10, or 40%.

Gross margin or gross profit is what is left over from net sales after the following are taken into account:

- The cost of the merchandise.
- Freight and other costs related to getting the merchandise to the store.
- Alterations and assembly.
- Discounts—a positive increase.
- Inventory shortage due to theft or accounting error.
- Markdowns due to soilage, season end, buying errors, employee discounts, and so on.

Gross margin is a critical figure in retailing because it is from gross margin dollars that all expenses such as wages and occupancy are paid. The right gross margin is a balancing act between:

- The store's profit path (high or low road).
- Cost of merchandise, competitive buying negotiations and so on.
- The right merchandise at the right time and in the right amount.
- The right service and promotional support to sell the merchandise.

Typically, stores with a gross margin percentage of less than 40% cannot do well in malls. The exceptions are those with a very high sales volume/high gross margin *dollar* approach to retailing, whose rent reflects this and is based on a dollar-per-square-foot rate rather than a typical percentage rent per square foot.

Expenses. When looking at the retailer's costs of doing business in your shopping center, be aware that there are really only three critical expense categories to be managed— wages, occupancy, and, to a lesser extent, advertising.

Wage/salary expenses are a retailer's single largest and most variable expense and therefore the most critical—they are also the most controllable. No typical high-road "A" retailer in your mall can make money, survive, and grow if total wages—including home office/owner wages and professional services—are more than 20% of sales. Store owners often do not include their own salary in the wage expense category, but instead take it out of profits. They are just deluding themselves. It is all right not to take a cash draw, but a "paper salary" for the owner-operator should be shown in wage expenses for proper analyses of wage costs.

Typically, wage costs by function are:

- Sales and sales related: 8–11%
- Management and administration: 5–7%
- Other: 2–7%

Low-margin "B" stores will have proportionately lower wage percentages.

Profitable retailers typically have at least a 40/60 ratio of regular to part-time staff. They schedule staff by the hour and day—not by week and month. Smart retailers know that paying minimum wage usually means staffing with minimum-effort people. Good stores:

1. Pay more to get the best.
2. Train, train, train.
3. Motivate and reward.
4. Run a disciplined store.

Sales-effort clues to look for:

- Are there too many employees on hand at opening time and not enough during peak hours?

- Is there a manager visibly in the store and on duty at peak times?
- Are training/motivating sessions held before or after the store opens or closes?
- Is there low turnover of good staff and management?

Store-occupancy expense is the second-largest expense category and includes such items as rent, common area maintenance (CAM) costs, utilities, and taxes. A typical mall store cannot be profitable if occupancy costs exceed 12% of sales. Since this guideline varies with the type of commodity, it must be adjusted for very high or very low gross margin stores.

Occupancy costs should not be thought of entirely as fixed rates. Many progressive shopping center developers work hard to:

1. Reduce the center's administrative management expenses.
2. Build high-quality facilities to conserve energy.
3. Reduce store sizes and force higher sales productivity— often with very positive results.
4. Promote and advertise effectively to build traffic and sales.

Occupancy clues to look for:

- Can the store be downsized without loss of sales?
- Are all CAM costs, utilities, and advertising used productively?

Advertising can be the third major cost, and includes sales promotion, special events, special packaging and wrap (or all communications). All advertising and promotion should have an objective: to create store awareness, to build an image, to create immediate sales, or another business goal. Merchants should be encouraged to view good, consistent communication as an investment rather than an expense. They should be urged to get co-op advertising from suppliers in order to increase the pool of promotional funds. Typical advertising and promotional expenses will run from 2% to 5% of sales.

Advertising clues to look for:

- Is the advertising targeted at a specific consumer segment?
- Is the approach used consistently, not changed from year to year?
- Are all elements related to each other?

Other expenses should all be managed carefully. Unlike the development industry, retailing profits tend to be slimmer and depend on nickel-and-dime expense control on the part of a cost-conscious store manager.

THE IMPORTANCE OF INVENTORY MANAGEMENT

The retailer's goal should be to have enough inventory to meet demand yet not so much that investment and holding costs become excessive, or markdowns eliminate gross margin. A system to manage inventory is needed for three reasons:

1. Financial—to keep the dollar investment in merchandise within budget.
2. Operational—to ensure a proper balance between fast-and-slow-selling stock-keeping units (SKUs).
3. Strategic—to keep a focus on the shape or direction of inventory offerings to shoppers.

In order to manage unit/SKU turnover and thus ensure the right inventory, an owner/manager must have a formal inventory system of unit control that is used in a disciplined way. This permits management to take action both on slow sellers—through markdowns, regroupings, and so on—and on fast sellers—by reordering, placement in high-traffic locations such as near the cash register, and so on.

There are three possible types of control:

1. Physical counting of inventory at regular intervals; for example, weekly recording of stock-on-hand in relation to the initial inventory, and estimating rate of sales.

2. Perpetual inventory count from individual receipts and sales of merchandise.
3. Information captured at the point of sale (POS) and calculated electronically with modern cash register and management information systems, which is now within the financial means of all retailers.

Inventory turnover (TO) is a measure of buying, sales, and inventory management efficiency. It is calculated by the simple formula:

$$\frac{\text{retail sales}}{\text{average inventory @ retail}} = \text{turnover (TO)}$$

$$\frac{\$360,000 \text{ sales}}{\$120,000 \text{ in inventory}} = 3 \text{ turns or } 3 \text{ TO}$$

Some typical turnovers are shown in the table that follows. It should be noted that these are typical figures. Successful retailers will have turnovers 50% to 100% higher.

Maximizing inventory productivity. In order to develop a successful merchandising operation, which often results in increased inventory turnover, retailers must develop a strategy of high-focus merchandising. This is a straightforward concept which matches up the merchandise assortment with the needs, wants, and desires of the store's target customer segment. This usually results in a reduction of the number of classifications the store will stock. It is very difficult for an owner/operator to do a good job on more than three to five classifications, yet many retailers are trying to be a department store in 1,200 square feet.

Inventory management clues to look for:

- Does the store have an inventory control system?
- Is it used regularly?
- Is the store using (or planning to use) a computer for inventory control?
- Is there a steady flow of merchandise into the store, rather than peaks and valleys?

TYPICAL INVENTORY TURNOVER

	Department Store	Independent Specialty Store	Chain Specialty Store
Fast-food	—	30.0	35.0
Women's clothing	5.0	4.0	5.5
Men's clothing	3.0	2.5	4.0
Personal needs and small wares	3.0	2.5	3.5
Cosmetics, fragrances, toiletries, drugs	3.0	2.5	3.2
Electronic audiovisual appliances, music, records	3.0	2.5	3.3
Shoes	2.5	2.0	2.8
Sporting goods	2.5	2.0	2.7
Home furnishings and furniture	2.2	2.0	2.5

- Is there prompt markdown action on slow sellers and repeats of fast sellers?
- Does the store limit itself to a few merchandise classifications, rather than being "all over the map"?

PURCHASING

The buying trip, often thought of as the fun or romantic part of retailing, is actually the reverse. It is—or should be—long, hard days of detailed preparation and intense concentration on what and what not to buy. The actual selection of an item or style is the last step in the activity. Some successful retail buying factors are:

1. A merchandise budget.
2. A buying plan.

3. Purchasing.
4. An even flow of merchandise.
5. Sales targets.
6. An analysis of every supplier.
7. An evaluation of your store's performance.

A merchandise budget should be prepared four to six months prior to the selling season. It should be based on a history of previous sales and markdowns so that shipping dates can be correctly developed in response to customer wants rather than manufacturers' production schedules.

A buying plan should be developed showing how the amounts allocated in the merchandise budget are to be spent. For each classification, the price lines and manufacturers should be detailed. The plan should support the store's strategic marketing position.

Purchasing should take place only after a budget with a supportive buying plan has been developed. Then a dollar "open-to-buy" control system should be set up to avoid over-buying or underbuying.

An even flow of merchandise throughout the season can be ensured if the buyer makes plans to receive merchandise monthly. Each individual order should also be written by month to avoid shipments that are too early or too late.

Sales targets are crucial, and can be developed either top-down or bottom-up. Top-down targets take into account market share and sales productivity aims along with economic trends. Bottom-up targets take into account history plus trend for each classification.

Analyze every supplier thoroughly at the end of each season for:

- Units sold as a percent of units received.
- Units received relative to units ordered.
- Units not sold at regular, full markup price.
- Late shipments.

With this information, a retailer can cut back weak performers and build strong performers.

Evaluate past performance. Stores should conduct a quarterly evaluation of the previous three-month period in order to make future plans. The evaluation should be done immediately after each selling quarter, while the information is still fresh.

Buying practice clues to look for:

- Does the store have buying plans for each season?
- Does the manager have dollar open-to-buy controls? In use?
- Are frequent short trips to market taken rather than fewer long ones?
- Does the buyer spend an extra day to see the stores and get new ideas? Lines? Motivation?

NONFINANCIAL TROUBLE INDICATORS

Often a retailer will not share financial information with center management. However, there are other ways to discover that a retailer is in financial trouble and may need help. Some visible danger signs are:

1. A perpetual sale or clearance sign—the retailer is desperately buying sales volume.
2. Slow rent payment—shows lack of cash flow.
3. Lack of inventory depth—there are no funds for normal purchases.
4. Lack of best-sellers or empty shelf space—suppliers may have stopped shipping because of nonpayment.
5. Firing of good staff—to "save" payroll and replace with minimum-wage staff.
6. A lot of old inventory—fear of taking markdowns. This last problem occurs when a store is afraid the bank will notice the drop in inventory assets and gross margins on the store's statements and reduce the size of its operating loan.

In contrast, a store that is doing well will show clear signs of discipline such as:

1. Opening on time.
2. Cleanliness.

3. Good visual presentation, signs.

4. A good in-depth stock of basics and best-sellers.

5. Well-dressed and motivated staff.

6. Systems to monitor performance.

7. A clear focus on the target customer.

John Williams is president of John C. Williams Consultants Ltd., a Toronto-based retail marketing, planning, and market research company which, in addition to other activities, provides shopping center developers with retail workshops, merchant counseling, advice on merchant mix, and revitalization and marketing plans. Mr. Williams is a member of the International Council of Shopping Centers and has spoken at the organization's conventions. He is coauthor of the National Retail Merchants Association's and Retail Council of Canada's *Strategic Retail Marketing: How to Be a Winner; Christmas Planning & Ideas* workbooks; and, Heritage Canada's *Marketing Main Street.*

6

Advertising/ Promotion Tips For Retailers

• **Kenneth A. Banks,** Eckerd Drug Company

Many companies spend a lot of money on advertising. What makes some companies different is that they do their homework first and then stick with the strategies that they've developed, which means doing the same types of advertising— but differently—as a result of their findings. It means breaking away from the unimaginative advertising of most retailers, but always knowing why they are deviating from the norm.

Eckerd Drugs has grown from a corner drugstore in the 1950s to a $2.6 billion chain that fills well over a million prescriptions each week. One of the reasons for this growth has been the company's creative advertising and promotion policies. With advertising expenses of nearly $100,000,000 in 1986, Eckerd is today the most aggressive drugstore advertiser in the country. Our company's advertising dollars pay off because, from the beginning to the present, we have dared to be different.

Daring to be different means daring to break the rules. What I mean by rules are the "Eight Reasons Not to Be Different" that advertising people hear from CEOs, agencies, merchandise managers, and others. If you listen to these people and not to the customer, you will never be different. On examination, every one of those so-called reasons simply turns out to be bad advice.

EIGHT "RULES" TO BREAK

Bad Advice #1: Advertising makes the register ring.

The fact is that advertising does *not* make the register ring. It's customers that do—and finding out *why* and *how* they shop your store, and then encouraging them to come in, is what increases sales. For years Eckerd spent over 85% of its advertising dollars promoting sales. Although we were promoting drugstore items like aspirin and shampoo, our ads did not distinguish us from other large retailers.

We then did some intensive research on our customers. Talking to more than 3,000 of them via exit interviews, telephone interviews, and focus groups, we found that though we were advertising like a mass merchant, the customer didn't shop us like a mass merchant. Over 48% shopped for something they needed in a hurry. They came to us because we were convenient. Only 12% came to us for a specific advertised item. So we completely redid our promotional thinking and came up with a campaign that says, "Okay, customers, if you're busy and can't wait, we've got what you need."

We didn't use the research just to come up with a new ad campaign. We had to make our stores easier to shop as well. This meant remodeling nearly 300 stores in nine months, and while we were doing it we ran a spot ad that let our customers know the store changes were being made for them.

We're not the only people in Florida making good use of market research. One furniture chain noticed that sales were slowest during the pre-Thanksgiving and holiday period. Research indicated this could be a prime time for major furniture purchases because customers wanted their homes to look their best for holiday guests. Yet with all the confusion and hoopla, and special holiday delivery hours—made famous by department stores—the customer didn't feel it was worth the effort to shop for something that would not arrive until after the new year. The store, however, knew it could deliver before then and developed an ad that told its customers so. The spot had to be pulled after three days because it brought so much additional business the store figured it would *not* be able to keep its promise! That year, what was once the slowest month became the biggest month for sales.

Bad Advice #2: Listen to the ad experts!

Everyone from buyers to district merchandising managers think they know advertising. They're not experts, but they certainly do have opinions. So does the customer, and only the customer has real expertise.

Thirty years ago Jack Eckerd started a photo service that offered two prints of every shot every time, so that vacationers and travelers in Florida had copies to give to people at home. A massive promotion campaign led to seven full-time photo labs and over $100 million in sales each year. But the competition finally caught on and not only offered two prints at a lower price, they also offered a single-print choice at a ridiculously low price. The "experts" throughout our company saw the competition's ads and heard some customers say they didn't always want two prints, and suggested dropping the two-print program and changing to a cheap single-print program.

Fortunately, we checked with our customers first and found some interesting facts:

- Over 66% said Eckerd was their photo source.
- 80% knew our two-for-one program.
- 30% said quality was now the most important factor, up from 16% before.
- Only 24% said price was important, making that the number 3 factor.
- To almost everyone, the name Kodak meant quality.

The result was that we branded our program with Kodak and developed a series of ad spots promoting it.

Bad Advice #3: Do it like the competition.

Most advertisers do what the competition does, especially at Christmas time. The routine is for everybody to show some nice Christmas gift items, or easier yet, run a cosmetic vendor co-op spot with your logo superimposed on it and come up with a new Christmas slogan that sounds just like everyone else's.

Our research showed us that, despite 30 circulars and mailers over the previous two years, we were not thought of as a source for Christmas gifts. We were not recognized as a place for designer fragrances, even though we did more cosmetics business than some of the department stores in our markets. We also found that no matter how hard we tried in November and early December, business didn't take off until the last two weeks before the holiday.

The reason relates to the numbers mentioned earlier— 48% of our shoppers were in a hurry and found us convenient. After December 14 this became especially important as the number of shoppers rating convenience and time as the most important factors jumped to 60%. So we ran some different spots at Christmas—no items, Santas or slogans—just commonsense messages telling customers we were a convenient source for presents and could save them time during this busy season.

Bad Advice #4: Put all your efforts in print.

I am not saying, "Stop print advertising." Run-of-the-press advertising and circulars are still the backbone of retail promotional advertising. Just don't depend on them exclusively. The customer doesn't. Two cases may prove my point.

1. Every week we would advertise in print a sale on one brand of blank videotape or another. But sales were below our goals. So we did some extensive market research. Not only did we find that most of the tape customers only bought a blank when they needed one, we also learned that despite all those weekly ads only 8% even thought we carried tapes in our stores. So we went on the medium that the products were being used for—television—and ran a spot on our tapes

during the fall sweeps period that said we were close, convenient and had a sale as well.

2. A food combo store did some research and found that despite all the newspaper ads by every food store in the country, when asked, 82% of the customers said they preferred *everyday low prices* because it was more convenient, gave them more choice as to what they were shopping for each week, and in the long run saved them more of their food dollar. So the combo ran a new TV spot for customers who don't read the papers before they shop and provided a garbage bag named the "circular file" for other stores' circulars.

Bad Advice #5: Keep the store the same when business is down.

In many cases, the real reason business is not good is that the market has changed and the stores haven't changed with it. Why do so many retailers think the "oldies but goodies" will bring them back to the top of the hit parade again?

Several years ago, our photo-finishing sales began to slump, and before jumping into the price wars mentioned earlier, we looked at the industry figures which projected that by 1985, at least 50% of the pictures taken would be on 35mm film. We were already selling 35% of our film to 35mm camera owners, yet 35mm film accounted for only 22% of our processing. Again, we set out to ask the customer why, and the answer quickly emerged. "Look, I just spent $200 for a camera," the customer said. "I'm just not going to take the film to a drugstore for processing."

We set out to change that. First, we created a whole new package called Ultralab 35—a branded processing which was only available at Eckerd. Then we told the customer in a high-tech yet simple way that we were the ones to trust those award-winning photos to.

The results: Processing of 35mm film now equals film sales. Our roll volume is growing in a relatively flat industry, and even our business on the basic 110/disc snap shooter has improved due to the halo effect of the quality message.

Bad Advice #6: Keep the store the same when business is up.

Once again an example tells the story best. Our pharmacy business is the key to our sales and growth, and we don't need to do a lot of research to know that. But the way prescriptions are being filled today is changing. There are now many places that fill prescriptions, from mail-order catalogs to health-maintenance organizations. So we went back to the customers to see why they chose a pharmacy and what would keep them from switching. Over 90% said they went to the pharmacist—the person, not the store where the pharmacist worked—and 96% said they would follow that person's recommendation for health-related products. In fact, on a national survey, pharmacists were the second most trusted professionals, right behind the clergy.

So we doubled media spending on our pharmacists and we decided to highlight the extra things our pharmacists do. We told customers, "If our pharmacists go out of their way in these instances, think what they'll do for your routine prescription."

Bad Advice #7: Don't use an agency.

Why is it that the world's greatest advertisers—Procter & Gamble, Pepsi, Coca-Cola, Ford, McDonald's—all need the expertise of an agency, yet so many retailers think that they don't need any help? We use two agencies—first, because we aren't that smart, and second, to give us perspective. We all get too close to our businesses for our own good and sometimes we need to take a fresh look—take a step back—and a good agency can help do just that.

For two years our agency encouraged us to go out and buy a TV spot that was more expensive than anything we had ever run because we had such a great story to tell. Finally the head of our agency spoke to the chairman of our board and convinced him to run the spot. It won last year's Retail Ad of the Year Award. The award is nice, but the letters from our customers and our pharmacists are the real proof.

Bad Advice #8: Keep it simple, stupid (K.I.S.S.)

If this one deserves discussion, it is that consistent success comes only from a lot of hard work and staying in touch with your customers.

SIX RULES TO FOLLOW FOR SUCCESS

Don't rely on hearsay to formulate great advertising. When it comes to strategic planning and great creative work, doing your homework and talking directly to the customer on an ongoing basis is the only way you can dare to be different and dare to be successful. To summarize:

1. *Understand the market.* Research it; look at industry trends; talk to key suppliers; analyze the competition.
2. *Talk to the market.* Use focus groups, exit interviews, and telephone interviews. Find out whatever the customers want that they are not afraid to tell you.
3. *Excite the market.* Don't take the customer for granted. As an advertising great, Leo Burnett said, "Don't ever bore the reader or viewer of your ad." Their time is too precious for dumb advertising.
4. *Be different.* Be yourself. Stand out, but also be relevant and consistent with what the research is telling you.
5. *Analyze the results.* No matter how well you do all the other steps, you are going to make mistakes. Even if the ads do work, keep analyzing because the market changes more quickly than your creative staff can anticipate, so you better be ready.
6. *The customer comes first.* In strategic planning and market research this is not just a slogan. It's the only way to ensure that when you dare to be different you will be reaching the right customer.

Kenneth A. Banks is vice president for marketing communications for Eckerd Drug Company, a Florida-based chain with stores in shopping malls. Eckerd won the *Advertising Age* award for the top TV retail commercials in 1984 and 1985, Retail Advertising Conference awards for both TV and radio in 1985 and 1986, and the top campaign award at the International Film Festival in New York City in 1987.

7

Training:
The Route to
Increased Sales

• **Pamela Muston,** Melvin Simon & Associates, Inc.

One way for mall developers and managers to increase the sales of their center is by providing a sales program for the center's retailers. Although national retailers tend to have their own in-house sales program, not every chain manager has had formal training in how to train others. Furthermore, depending on the center's geographic location and the size of the chain manager's area, some stores don't receive frequent visits from their supervisor. Such stores are naturally receptive to additional sales training. Both department stores and national chains (which do have very good programs) have participated in programs for enhancing selling skills that we developed at Melvin Simon & Associates.

The programs we have in place include "$elling!," a $elling newsletter, Secret Shop, and $ell Star. The $elling program, the first to be developed, is a very basic presentation designed to supplement and/or reinforce the most common sales training principles. It consists of six steps:

1. How to approach customers.
2. How to discover customer wants and needs.
3. How to present merchandise and create a desire to buy.
4. How to handle customer objections.
5. How to close the sale.
6. How to suggestion-sell.

Each step is defined and discussed and examples are given. Role-playing is then used to reinforce each step. The example that follows combines the best features of these programs.

SELLING BASICS

A basic selling program starts with preparation. It involves:

- *Appearing professional.* Look like the expert you are. Smile and be enthusiastic.
- *Knowing your merchandise.* Check every day for changes in stock. Read product tags for care instructions, warranties, etc. Try on or use products to determine quality. Be aware of advertising selling points.
- *Establishing a genuine relationship with the customer.* Use common sense, sincerity, and creativity.

Customer approach is the second step. Be sure to:

- Know when and how to approach customers. Give them a chance to stop and look at the merchandise first.
- Use a greeting and apply your product knowledge.

Two types of approaches are the:

1. *Greeting*—"Good afternoon. That's one of our most popular items."
2. *Merchandise*—"I see you're interested in _____"; describe what the customer is looking at.

Once the approach has been made, it is time to sell the product, keeping in mind the following basics:

1. Use *who, what, where, when, how,* and *why* during the selling conversation.
2. Observe facial expressions. Look directly into the customer's eyes.
3. Confirm your understanding of what the customer is looking for.

4. Never show more than three items. Remove items the customer is not interested in.
5. Get the customer involved with the merchandise. Let the customer touch, feel, smell, taste, or hear the product.
6. Demonstrate the merchandise and its features.

Customers are bound to raise objections with regard to the merchandise itself, its price, and the time to buy. There is an answer to each type of objection:

- Price—tell the customer about different ways to pay: cash, charge, layaway, and so on.
- Merchandise—reconfirm customer needs, ask more questions, and again point out product features and benefits.
- Time—describe the store's return policy; stress *now* is the time to buy, especially during the gift-giving season.

Closing the sale involves more basics:

1. *Never* walk away and leave the final decision to the customer. Help the customer make a decision by giving your opinion.
2. *Don't* rush the customer. Let all customers know they are important.
3. *Remove* items of no interest. Narrow the choices.
4. *Ask* open-ended questions about the choices, such as "What do you like about the item?"
5. *Suggest* a method of payment.

Suggestive selling now comes into play. To suggest-sell means to:

- "Plant a seed"—while showing the primary purchase, suggest related items.
- "Add on" items—after a decision has been made on the primary item, suggest items that complement the purchase such as accessories for a dress or a maintenance agreement on an appliance.

Part of an effective sales training program is a list of suggested phrases and questions to use while presenting the merchandise and closing the sale. Phrases that present merchandise might include:

- This is one of the most popular styles we have.
- This is one of the season's most important colors.
- This is one of the newest items; it just arrived today (this week).
- This was featured in our current advertising.
- This is one of the most versatile items (colors, for instance) you can buy.

AUGMENTATION

To provide our centers with longer-term results, Melvin Simon & Associates, Inc. has implemented several other programs to complement the $elling! program and to provide ongoing sales training.

1. We have expanded our $elling! program to include videos relating to each step. These videos enable sales training to be presented on a monthly basis. Modules can either be self taught or leader led. They can be presented at a large, total-center meeting or at a small category meeting, or used by individual retailers for store meetings. Retailers are asked to evaluate each session to provide immediate feedback and suggest other subjects to address.
2. A special newsletter has been developed that is sent to the center monthly. It features a different $elling! step each month, with discussion questions and exercises to reinforce the information. Monthly evaluations completed by center management provide measurable results.
3. Centers are currently conducting at least one "Secret Shop" during the year (most have two to four). Our Secret Shoppers are local customers who are asked to evaluate the center's customer service level based on our "Six Steps to $elling!" Each store is shopped three different times by three different shoppers. Stores are rated on a scale of one to five for each step and results are given to our retailers.

4. Sell Star, a holiday sales training video, is provided to our retailers during the fourth quarter. This 20-minute video provides an excellent tool for training new hires and/or temporary holiday staff, while at the same time reinforcing the Six Steps to $elling.

To measure the results a specific sales training program has had on a center, we rely on certain data, such as:

1. Participation numbers.
2. Sales reports.
3. Program evaluations.
4. Secret Shop results.

Together, these facts enable us to identify weaknesses in the selling process and to customize the training program to meet an individual center's needs. Category meetings are one area where retailers can concentrate on improving a specific skill. A presentation can then be developed to strengthen that skill.

PRESENTATION

Sales training programs are effective tools for a center to use in increasing sales when they:

1. Are professionally produced and provide materials that can be taken home.
2. Provide the center with an ongoing sales training program.
3. Are cost-effective.
4. Are structured so that various options for presenting the program are available.

Our experience has shown us that a single presentation provides only short-term sales increases. However, there are some situations where a one-time presentation is effective. These include:

1. Grand openings.
2. Re-grand openings.
3. Renovations.
4. New ownership.

A center cannot just announce a sales training program and expect the retailers to respond. A simple memo will just get "filed" in the wastebasket. We send a professionally produced brochure to our retailers six weeks prior to our $elling program. The mailing is sent to owners, corporate office personnel, regional/district managers, and store managers. The brochures generate about a 20% response rate. Then our center staff goes to work "selling" the training program.

Among the methods employed to encourage retailer attendance are:

- One-on-one communication with the store manager.
- Center newsletter articles.
- Merchant meetings, centerwide and category.
- Announcements at board meetings.
- Follow-up phone calls.
- Press releases sent to local radio stations and newspapers.

FURTHER BENEFITS

An important feature of the training programs is to encourage an exchange of ideas among retailers. During the sessions, it is customary to recognize one or two successful store managers. They will usually share their experiences, which then leads to a discussion on low-cost in-store sales boosters.

Comments from program evaluations also give us continuous feedback on what our retailers need. Suggested topics for programs in other areas have included:

- Visual merchandising.
- Displays.
- Signing.
- How to handle upset customers.
- How to interview.
- Promotion ideas.

Both our mall managers and marketing directors attend the training sessions. This not only increases their retail awareness but also demonstrates their commitment to improving center sales. The mall managers are then able to follow up on suggestions discussed during the meeting, while the marketing directors strive to merchandise sales-improving center events. This involvement positions our center staff as sales-oriented and strengthens the commitment on both sides, retailer and mall management, to achieve their common goal: increased sales.

Pamela Muston is a retail consultant at Melvin Simon & Associates, Inc., an Indianapolis-based real estate developer. The firm manages 60 million square feet of space in 39 states and is one of the largest shopping center developers, with 130 shopping facilities in 25 states. Prior to joining Melvin Simon & Associates in 1985, Ms. Muston worked for a national junior speciality chain for 15 years.

8

Special Techniques for Merchant Motivation

- Charlotte Ellis, CMD, Lehndorff USA Limited
- Edie Crane, CMD, David Hocker & Associates
- Carol L. Zimmer, Forbes/Cohen Properties
- Liz Coleman-Napoli, CMD, Riverside Square
- Karen R. Samford, CMD, Herring Marathon Group
- Betty Konarski, C.M. Enterprises, Inc.
- Jane A. Secola, CMD, Enterprise Development Co.

Mystery Shopper Programs

• Charlotte Ellis, CMD, Lehndorff USA Limited

People talk. They tell their friends when they are treated badly in a retail store. They also tell their friends when they receive excellent service offered by a competent salesperson who goes "the extra mile." And, because people talk about the service they receive in a particular mall, the professional managers of both the mall *and* the retail store should be curious about what those people are saying. A strong mystery shopper program assists merchants and mall management in offering excellent customer service, thus increasing the odds that when people talk, they will say only positive things about your mall and its stores.

Studies show that nearly 70% of the customers who stop patronizing a specific store or mall do so because an employee was uninterested or apathetic; no one seemed concerned whether or not the customer made a purchase. Often, the store owner doesn't see this poor performance, because of his high profile among store managers, and the mall management team is not generally treated as an average shopper would be. This makes it difficult for managers and marketing directors to evaluate a store's personnel with objectivity. Anonymity is required for a true picture of a day in the life of that store.

Anonymity is the hallmark of a mystery shopper program. Mystery shopper reports can make merchants aware of their store's actual service level.

Two options exist when a mall selects mystery shoppers. One option is the employment of community group members requiring funds for a project. The mall makes a donation to the organization in exchange for regular mystery shopper visits and reports. The second option is the use of a professional shopper service.

When the budget is a critical factor, creating a mystery shopper program from community groups is a solution. Unfortunately, the information received may not be without bias. These mystery shoppers come to their job with a history of perceptions about your mall and its stores. They probably already have natural biases, perhaps from having friends who work in the mall. Also, their information may not be gathered objectively. This option may, however, be the only affordable one for the mall.

When a more generous budget is available for a mystery shopper program, a professional shopper service is the preferred option. Professional mystery shoppers are trained observers who come to the task without prejudice. Furthermore, the professional shopper service knows which U.S. bench marks to judge your stores against. The service also often offers merchant seminars as a follow-up to individual store reports.

Whether a community group or a professional service is used, it's important to advise the merchants that a mystery shopper program is being undertaken. Tell the merchants how long the program will run and what aspects of the store's service performance will be evaluated. Anticipation of mystery shopper visits, after all, will improve customer service—and that's the point of the whole program.

Stores should be evaluated in a number of service areas, including employees' sales performance and professionalism, and the interior and exterior appearance of the business.

The mystery shopper should rate the following areas for sales performance:

- The length of time that elapsed before the shopper was greeted.
- The employee's efforts to sell product benefits.
- The employee's efforts to help the shopper make a decision.
- The employee's efforts to suggest additional merchandise to accompany a purchase.
- The employee's efforts to close the sale.
- The employee's courtesy and whether the customer was thanked irrespective of a positive buying decision.

The mystery shopper must also notice and evaluate the personal appearance and conduct of the store's employees:

- Were the employees dressed appropriately for work in that store?

- Were employees eating, drinking, smoking, or conducting personal phone conversations?
- Were the employees quick to extend a cordial greeting?
- How were dressing room security and fitting assistance handled?

The mystery shopper then evaluates the store's appearance and merchandising effectiveness. The major items to look for include:

- The cleanliness of the storefront and the interior, including fixtures and merchandise.
- The ease of access both into and within the store.
- The quality of the signage.
- The effectiveness of window and in-store displays.

While sales performance, employee performance, and store appearance measurements are sufficient for apparel and specialty stores, restaurants and food service businesses require still another area of evaluation.

Mystery shoppers should ask the following questions about food providers:

- Was the food handled properly?
- Did the food look and taste good?
- Was change given correctly?
- Was the restaurant (or food court) clean, including tables, napkin holders, ashtrays, and sugar, salt, and pepper dispensers?
- Was the noise level acceptable?
- Were the counters clean and neat?

After the evaluation is completed and scores are tabulated (a scale of 100 is easiest for all to understand), the mall management team should review it with the store owner and manager in a positive, not accusative, fashion. Everyone benefits when customer service improves, so the information provided by mystery shoppers should be presented as good news. Reevaluation should also take place to measure improvement.

Just as the initial report was, this information should be shared with owners, managers, and home offices.

Merchant seminars, motivation programs, and incentive awards should be offered to help managers improve their employees' performance. These aids promote a goal-oriented team effort to improve the mall's overall rating on customer service.

Probably because mall management personnel are also customers, they often have valid complaints about the lack of customer service retailers extend. A mystery shopper program is the first step toward improving the situation. Nothing can be more important. The performance of a salesperson in any store in your mall is critical in forming customer perceptions of the mall. A negative experience at the cash terminal can negate award-winning architecture, a top-drawer tenant mix, an enviable location, and great marketing. A positive experience can only enhance those features.

Charlotte Ellis, CMD, is vice president of marketing for the Lehndorff USA group of companies in Dallas, Texas. Since 1974, she has been involved in shopping center marketing and advertising. She is currently responsible for the marketing programs of Lehndorff's nine regional centers, 13 community centers, 36 office buildings, as well as the company's corporate advertising and public relations. She has also served on the faculty of the International Council of Shopping Centers' Marketing Institute.

Incentive Programs

• **Edie Crane, CMD,** David Hocker & Associates

An effective method of motivating merchants is a Mall Incentive Program. Too often retailers neglect the proper training of store managers and sales associates or fail to recognize and reward outstanding personnel. If positive reinforcement for a job well done is lacking in-store, it can be provided by mall management.

In 1985, University Mall in Carbondale, Illinois, was definitely in a slump. The economy, based mainly on coal and agriculture, was suffering; new competition in the form of a larger mall in a nearby town was luring customers; and the morale of the merchants was low.

Working with an astute board of directors, the marketing director analyzed the situation. Merchandising events and promotions were in top form and advertising media and positioning were satisfactory. However, though the number of customers had not decreased noticeably, the dollars those customers were spending had decreased. It soon became evident that since there were fewer dollars to be had, the merchants had to make every customer count.

In the months that followed, a retail committee appointed by the board put together a motivational program for the University Mall merchants. The program kicked off in May 1985 with three days of sales motivation and training seminars for managers, associates, and non-selling personnel. Additional ongoing seminars on in-store promotion, shoplifting, customer service, merchandising, etc., were also scheduled. Quality circles for the various merchandise categories were established so that merchants could help one another by discussing methods of improving sales for the entire category. The final motivational aspect, a mall incentive program, was designed by a merchant committee. The program was instituted for a six-month trial period.

The incentive awards were presented monthly to top achievers as well as those employees who maintained the best sales performance throughout the mall's incentive program. The monthly awards were given to the:

1. Top Store—a traveling trophy was used.
2. Top Manager—in the mall—received $100, press coverage, and a commendatory letter sent to the home office.
3. Top Manager—for each category—received $50, press coverage, and a commendatory letter to the home office.
4. Top Employee—for each category—received $25.
5. Top Employee—from each store—received a movie pass, dinner for two (or some other award), and a certificate of merit.

The first three award categories above were based on the percentage of sales increase over the previous year's sales. The top employee in each category was selected from the same store as the top manager of the category. Top employees from each store were selected by their store managers.

Two awards were given out for performance based on the entire six months of the program:

1. Top Manager—in the mall—received $500, press coverage, and a commendatory letter to the home office.
2. Top Employee—received $100 and a commendatory letter to the home office.

The top manager in the mall was selected based on his/her sales-increase percentage over the previous year's sales, whereas the top employee was most frequently selected as a category top employee as well. The cost of the incentive awards breaks down as shown below:

Monthly Awards:

1 Top Manager	$100
5 Top Category Managers	$250
6 Top Employees	$150
	$500

$500 x 6 months = $3,000

Program Awards:

1 Top Manager	$500
1 Top Employee	$100
	$600

Total Cost:
  $3,000 + $600 = $3,600

The program's results were impressive. The truly outstanding managers and sales associates doubled their previous performances. The additional publicity received by the mall in local media increased merchant pride and the letters written by mall developer David Hocker to the various home offices resulted in increased recognition for the outstanding employees.

Mistakes were made, however. An incentive program should not be based on sales increases alone. Other factors equally important to retail success should be considered. Store cleanliness, merchandise display, participation in mall events, and advertising are also good judging criteria and would allow for recognition of a larger number of merchants. Additional encouragement for merchants who did not win should have been provided. At one point during the program, since the same managers won again and again, enthusiasm waned. Finally, although appreciated, cash awards were not as important as anticipated. The publicity and recognition within the community and by store home offices were much more valued than expected.

An incentive program, like any other program in a mall, is successful only if the merchants support it. For that reason, it is wise to include successful merchants in the planning group. Not only can they help design the program, but they also become prime advocates in the mall for the program.

Edie Crane, CMD, is vice president of marketing for David Hocker & Associates in Owensboro, Kentucky, which has developed 30 centers containing 7 million square feet of shopping space. Mr. Crane has had extensive experience establishing and supervising marketing programs which include motivational and incentive programs.

Category Teams

- Carol L. Zimmer, Forbes/Cohen Properties

Category teams are groups of merchants organized from specific merchandise categories for the purpose of self-motivation and increased sales. As Lansing Mall management analyzed sales-producing events in the centers, it became increasingly apparent that smaller, targeted activities paid off more often than large-scale events with limited participation.

Grouping merchants together by "category" has the advantage of creating sales. Participants take advantage of economies of scale, like savings in production, while maximizing sales during peak selling periods and fulfilling a lease requirement in the process.

Participation is achieved by forming category teams. At Lansing Mall, a major campaign was planned with four categories—jewelry, shoes, men's apparel, and ladies' apparel—representing the largest percentage of sales in the 125-store mall.

The initial meeting was held over lunch with merchants from each category. The agenda was introductory and informative in nature with mall management in charge of the proceedings.

First on the agenda was a report from the marketing director on future fashion trends for the specific category. This information was obtained from visits and calls to New York City, buying office conversations, and from general and specialized fashion publications. The expectation was for merchants to adjust or realign stock levels based on new information.

Each store manager also received individual store sales information, along with their store's rank in total sales volume and in dollar sales per square foot compared to the category totals. This gave the merchants an idea of how their store was performing in its category. To assist them in creating sales, the management team then reviewed many of the centerwide events which are designed to produce traffic. Each received a list and information on the services provided by the center and were encouraged to take advantage of them for sales increases. These included fashion shows, informal modeling, display cubes, fashion panel use, gift guides and tie-in promotional events.

Finally, at this and subsequent meetings, a general discussion was held aimed at helping each category create more sales at the center. From the outset, it was explained that no one was expected to reveal any secrets, which seemed to relax the store managers and later opened them up to brainstorming together. To spark conversation we asked such questions as:

- How, if you are a multistore operation, do your sales here compare with your sales at other centers?
- What kinds of promotions have created sales in your store in the past?
- What can we do to make our center *the* place to shop for your category's merchandise?

This last question generates the most discussion on creating special events specific to categories. At this point it is important to mention that the management team should come prepared with a plan for an event. Otherwise, every store has it's own idea of what might work for them specifically and a consensus is extremely hard to achieve. Listen to your retailers comments, however, especially those related to timing, and make adjustments as needed.

When reviewing the program the following topics should be addressed:

- Goals and objectives for the category effort.
- The promotion's theme.
- Timing—What are the category's peak periods? Should promotions coincide with the peak periods or be held at other times?
- On-mall activities to create excitement and interest in the category.
- In-store activities to create sales for individual stores.

- A co-op advertising package with a multimedia approach— radio, newspaper, in-store collateral materials, direct-mail postcards.
- Deadlines and responsibilities for each store and for the mall's marketing department.
- A date for the next meeting.

The results of the meetings, and the plans made, varied from category to category. The jewelry category decided to center their promotion around diamonds. An event was planned, "Designs in Diamonds," featuring a gift giveaway and contest, with prizes donated by the stores. A fashion panel distributed some 2,000 cubic zirconiums (diamond look-alikes) throughout the center over a three-day period in April before the peak Mother's Day shopping season in May. Hidden among the stones were real ¼-carat diamonds. Customers had to take the gift to a designated store to find out if they'd gotten a real diamond.

Individual jewelers also planned in-store activities such as remount clinics, visits from guest jewelry designers, or free inspection and cleaning of jewelry. The excitement and traffic generated in each store could then be capitalized on to create sales. Co-op advertising plans for the promotion included newspaper, posters (in-store and on-mall), postcards direct-mailed to the jewelers' mailing lists, and promotional cards attached to each gift package.

The shoe category chose the August "Back-to-School" peak period. Among the activities planned were a shoe fashion show, freeze-modeling by children in focal points of the center, and a major contest in which one lucky shopper could win a wardrobe of shoes for the whole family. Each store created its own in-store excitement with trunk shows, giveaways, and modeling. Advertising media included radio, posters, post-cards, and in-store flyers.

The men's wear category chose to tie in with Father's Day and a classic car show. Activities encompassed a fashion show and informal modeling in and around the automobile exhibits. Customers could receive a gift with purchase ("Dad" key chain) by presenting their receipt for $20 or more from participating men's stores. Co-op advertising took the form of newspaper ads, postcards, posters, and contest "playing cards" distributed in the mall.

The ladies' apparel promotion was planned for a traditional "Men's Night" during the holiday selling period. It featured entertainment, free gift wrapping for all male customers, an information center ready with gift suggestions, minifashion shows and Mylar balloons in each ladies' store window. In-store activity included trunk shows, informal modeling and personal shoppers. Advertising appeared as print ads, a ladies' direct-mail piece, posters and in-store flyers.

In many cases, peer pressure helped achieve 100% merchant participation in category events. Participation requirements included:

- Purchasing the agreed-upon advertising package.
- Creating an in-store activity that brings traffic and sales to individual stores.
- Providing a giveaway consistent with the program.
- Supporting the in-store event to guarantee its success.

Total participation in the event fulfilled one advertising lease requirement per each merchant's lease.

Creating events for specific categories of merchants is a rewarding, quantifiable use of merchants' association dollars. Merchants are often surprised at the center's interest and knowledge in their category efforts and seem committed to the success of an event planned just for them. Lansing Mall has high hopes for future, collective category events and their ability to increase merchant sales.

Carol L. Zimmer is the corporate marketing director for Forbes/Cohen Properties, Southfield, Michigan. Recently promoted, Ms. Zimmer began her shopping center career with Forbes/Cohen as marketing director of the Lansing Mall, a regional center with 125 stores in Lansing, Michigan.

The Annual Meeting

• Liz Coleman-Napoli, CMD, Riverside Square

An annual meeting should be carefully planned to achieve specific goals. The underlying goals for our meetings are:

1. To motivate merchants to improve their operations and to increase sales
2. To provide important information regarding operational policies and management procedures
3. To encourage merchant participation in center advertising and special events by introducing the upcoming year's advertising and promotional schedule and generating enthusiasm for it.

Once the goals are established, select an appropriate location, time, and theme. Choosing the correct ambiance for the meeting is important. Center management must be sensitive to the situation of the retailers. If times are hard, a country club dinner with all the trimmings is not appropriate; however, if times are good, an elegant dinner may be in order. A no-frills meeting, on the other hand, may not give the event proper significance and may make it indistinguishable from monthly merchants' association marketing information meetings. An elegant and appropriately festive breakfast is often more convenient and cost-efficient than a cocktail party or dinner. Whatever the situation, the right balance must be found.

Timing is also a key factor. The meeting should take place at least six to eight weeks before the beginning of the promotional year so that retailers have ample time to budget and plan for participation in the events.

The key to successfully motivating merchants through an annual meeting, however, is the choice of a compelling theme. Our theme is selected at corporate headquarters with input from the field. "$ell" (1983), "Compete" (1984), "The

Best" (1985), and "Information" (1986) were successful themes at our annual meetings.

To encourage a large turnout, especially of decision makers, attractive invitations are sent to store owners, managers, home-office principals, and advertising personnel. Each invitation is followed up with an additional contact to ensure maximum attendance.

Our center is in an affluent but toughly competitive Northeastern environment. Meetings begin with an overview of both national and local retailing, followed by an awards ceremony recognizing the sales performances of the previous year's winners and then by the introduction of the new year's theme.

The year of the "Compete" theme, eight "Oscars"— personalized trophies copied from the Hollywood originals— were awarded to the previous year's winning merchants for the highest percentage increase in sales in such categories as shoes, men's apparel, and gifts. Other centers held contests for the highest sales per square foot in a category.

Each participant at every annual merchant meeting receives a kit which introduces the theme and contains thematic material for the merchant to use throughout the entire year. The kit also contains general information about the operation of the retail center as well as specific marketing and advertising materials. Through a commitment agreement form, merchants can confirm their participation in the mall's advertising program. Also included in the kit are idea note pads, on which managers and employees can make suggestions for improving their individual store operations, and adhesive-backed "Today's Item to Suggest" pads, designed for mounting on the cash register to remind employees of the special merchandise they can highlight to maximize sales.

To further involve and carry the theme to the employees, the store managers' kits also include special "Contest" pads for posting the results of in-store contests. "Employee of the Week" entry blanks are also provided as part of a monthly mallwide contest. During the "Compete" year, store managers were asked to enter their best store employee of the week into a drawing, with the winner receiving a monetary gift certificate redeemable at the mall stores.

The "Compete" spirit and momentum was established by holding two contests during the meeting in which participating merchants were urged to outdo each other, namely:

1. A markdown contest—Two merchants were asked to compute a 10% markdown on various items—the winner was the first to compute all of the correct answers.
2. A display contest—Two merchants were asked to change a table of disheveled shirts and sweaters into an attractive display—the winner was decided by audience applause.

Next, a slide presentation challenged managers to question the daily practices and policies of their stores by asking such questions as:

• Am I ever first?
• Do my employees care about how we did on their day off?
• What have I done to get better than my competition?

The "Compete" marketing segment, the heart of the program, began with a second slide presentation which explained its philosophy, reviewed the center's various market segments, to whom the "Compete" marketing plan was designed to appeal, and then detailed the program, event by event. The aim was to get the merchants thinking about how their merchandise could tie in with a centerwide sale, how they might obtain dollars from vendors for co-op advertising, and the like.

Since the theme was "Compete," merchants were encouraged to view their role as competitors from an aggressive new vantage point. They were reminded that not only do they compete with retail entities outside the mall, they also compete against their neighboring merchants—as well as within their own stores among their fellow associates. In addition, they also compete for share of market and share of advertising readership.

Presenting the coming year's marketing plan in conjunction with the theme and contests motivated the merchants to commit themselves to mall-sponsored advertising and special events. Also, as a direct result of the meeting, several merchants who were not required by lease to participate immediately agreed to sign on for the upcoming advertising schedule. Thus, the results achieved satisfied the initial objectives. Other well-planned meetings with similarly appropriate and thought-provoking themes, the right ambiance, and a touch of pizzazz have been equally successful in motivating merchants.

Liz Coleman-Napoli, CMD, is the general manager of Riverside Square, a JMB/Federated Realty center in Hackensack, New Jersey, with more than 90 fashion stores and restaurants. Ms. Coleman-Napoli has been a member of the International Council of Shopping Centers' Certified Marketing Director Committee and is a past chair of the organization's Eastern States Marketing Conference.

Sales Analysis

• Karen R. Samford, CMD, Herring Marathon Group

The fundamental responsibility of every mall management team is to increase retail sales. Consequently, an in-depth analysis of sales performance is absolutely essential. Preparation of this analysis is time-consuming but rewarding, for marketing directors and managers end up knowing more about their merchants' sales, category trends, overall mall performance, and, most significantly, the relationship between the marketing programs and mall sales.

The sales performance of all merchants in Herring Marathon Group's shopping malls are evaluated and analyzed in terms of retail productivity on a monthly basis. The format for their sales analysis has four components:

1. Summary of monthly sales: Provides monthly and year-to-date information on the dollars per square foot sold and percentage comparisons for both the center and categories.
2. Advertising/marketing philosophy: Justifies the target markets for each campaign and highlights those categories with an anticipated strong sales performance (that is, double-digit increases) as a result of the campaign.
3. Quantitative summary: Provides data on individual category sales as a percentage of overall center sales, as well as overage rent comparison in total dollars. Category sales summaries and individual category performances can pinpoint "strong" tenants and "weak" tenants and provide clues as to the *why* of their position. All this information can then be compared to trade area performance; that is, general market conditions and competitive centers.
4. Conclusion: Answers questions such as: Based on category and center performance, can a correlation be drawn between the marketing program and actual sales? How can the campaign be improved and should it be a part of future marketing plans?

Using the information derived from the summary of monthly sales and the advertising/marketing philosophy sections, one can cross-compare the high and low performance results to those results expected from the month's campaign.

If each management team is given an annual overage rent goal, the quantitative summary can be used to measure the success of center marketing efforts and alert the teams to problems and opportunities in sales performance. It can also be used to measure effectiveness. If, for example, $5,937 was spent in newspaper advertising to achieve $17,242 in percentage rent and prior lack of advertising had resulted in less percentage rent, the program could be considered successful. Performance may also be addressed qualitatively. For example, 15,000 direct-mail coupons were mailed, resulting in a +10% response for one food provider, its first increase in two months. And, another food provider was able to attribute losses of $10,000 to the recent opening of a McDonalds.

Lower sales performers are identified monthly and every effort is made to save these merchants. Emphasis, however, is placed on maximizing overage rent contenders. Using the quantitative summary and the center seasonality index to determine merchandise peaks allows further assistance planning to be done for a lagging category or for further improvement in a high producer's performance.

Category meetings are part of the annual management plan to share information on major merchandising campaigns and to solicit merchant support and input. Meetings are ideally held four to six months in advance of the merchandise season so that merchants can prepare for their involvement. Working with individual retailers is the next step in creating better retail programs. Herring Marathon's management teams use a Visual Store Evaluation (audit) to assist them in dealing constructively with a merchant. This tool addresses elements of a targeted store's operations, from merchandise presentation and salesmanship to housekeeping and display fixtures. Once the audit is performed by the team, a summary of the evaluation and recommendations are prepared for the follow-up meeting with the store manager. During this meeting, input from the store manager is added, then a summary of all findings and recommendations are sent to the district manager. Thereafter, assistance from the management team is directed at areas of needed improvement—whether improved customer relations or in-store promotions—for each merchant, and assistance programs are then designed by the management staff and merchant.

Involvement in the overall center management plan (that is, co-op advertising, events, quarterly seminars) is always a primary recommendation, as these plans are designed to increase sales for each category during its natural selling season. Quarterly seminars led by the management staff and an occasional guest speaker add to merchant momentum and keep everyone abreast of new tools and trends in the retail industry.

An effective follow-up to good retail programs for center merchants is the real key to positive results. Marketers must constantly evaluate programs implemented as they evaluate store performances. Once a merchant has been targeted for assistance, routine evaluations must be done, then shared with upper management.

Success stories should be touted in both monthly manager's reports (distributed to store managers) and quarterly reports mailed to corporate offices. Center programs designed to further improve sales are detailed in both communications long before they are to happen.

Analysis of retail performance should be constant. Tools such as the monthly sales analysis and visual store audit require a gradual educational process for both retailers and mall management. A retailer's success is ultimately based on long-range commitment, constant measuring of success and failure, and the flexibility to adapt, but a center management team armed with the right tools can really make a difference.

Karen Samford, CMD, is corporate marketing manager for Herring Marathon Group, Dallas, Texas, a firm specializing in an analytical approach to its marketing. She has been in the shopping center industry for seven years, is a former MAXI award winner, and conducted a 1987 International Council of Shopping Centers' Fall Conference session on marketing a group of centers as a package.

Incubators

• **Betty Konarski,** C.M. Enterprises, Inc.

"There is nothing so unequal as the equal treatment of unequals."

Why do shopping center managers seem to feel themselves morally bound to treat all new tenants alike? A much more equitable approach resulting in a higher success rate can be achieved by prescreening potential tenants, and locating those tenants who appear to be at high risk in *incubators*. More than 500 small business incubators now operate throughout the United States with success rates of 80% or higher. Many of the techniques which lead to this kind of success can be adapted by shopping centers.

An incubator combats the high failure rate of new businesses by reducing some of the obstacles that prevent them from getting inexpensive, appropriately sized space, access to commonly required administrative support services, and access to management, financial, and technical assistance. This can be achieved if the following considerations are taken into account.

INCUBATOR SPACE

1. Specifically select and set aside some space for start-ups.
2. Design under-market, short-term (1–2 years) lease terms with escalation clauses or percentage features to bring the tenant up to market within 3–5 years.
3. Establish annual check points so that the shopping center management team and the tenant work together toward success. After all, this makes for an equity partnership; the abated rent releases cash for inventory. Since most start-ups suffer from undercapitalization, this alone could be the boost that means the difference between success and failure. But don't stop there.

SHARED SERVICES

1. Identify a room which can be freed for use by your independent merchants.
2. Provide a copy machine, coffee pot, table and comfortable chairs, postage meter, dolly for transporting heavy items, and perhaps a sign-making machine.
3. Develop a reference library with copies of trade publications, local journals or chamber of commerce publications; plus business-related books like *Creating Excellence* by Craig R. Hickman and Michael A. Silva, *The One Minute Manager* by Kenneth Blanchard and Spencer Johnson, or *Minding the Store* by Stanley Marcus. Also, keep brochures from Small Business Administration seminars, Chamber of Commerce workshops, and all local small business seminars.
4. Jointly contract for: United Parcel Service pickup; a stamp machine; a person to do window and in-store displays; data processing, word processing, and secretarial help; and other services which are often too expensive for a single merchant to carry alone.
5. Arrange for the use of a conference room and/or small multipurpose room on an "as-available" basis for meetings with staff, wholesale representatives, or community leaders.
6. Sponsor monthly social gatherings or formal networking sessions, in which independent tenants can share information, sources, experiences, and support.

OUTSIDE RESOURCES

Community Colleges and Local Universities
Set up a working relationship with these local institutions. Invite their sponsorship of a workshop series or classes at the shopping center on subjects such as cash flow management, marketing, or whatever topics the tenants might find timely. If the school has a Small Business Institute, become

involved. Through this program, consulting teams of seniors in the School of Business Administration can provide a thorough business analysis for individual tenants who are willing to open their books.

Banks and Savings and Loan Associations

Bring in officers of local banks and savings and loan associations to determine who can offer the greatest amount of service to the center's small business merchants. Then, advise the merchants to individually and collectively establish their accounts with the financial institution that provides the best and most comprehensive service. Pooling accounts can reduce bank card costs and provide better backing for inventory loans. The clout is even greater if the center joins in with its own account.

Consultants

Contract with one or more local consulting firms to offer services for the merchants at the shopping center at no cost or at a reduced cost. Note that seminars on loan packaging and balance sheets coupled with an ongoing relationship with the financial institutions and consultants selected provide merchants with valuable survival tools.

INCUBATOR CANDIDATES

If a potential or existing tenant does not meet one or two of the following criteria, the store is definitely a candidate for an incubator. If three or more criteria are not met, the merchant is not a viable candidate for the shopping center.

1. Is the merchant an experienced or inexperienced business owner? First-time business owners represent a high failure risk category and thus make likely incubator candidates.
2. Does the merchant have a business plan? Ask to see it and look for two key elements. Is the capitalization adequate? Are there any methods in place to monitor performance?

3. What is the merchant's credit history? Call a few of the suppliers to determine whether there has been a problem.
4. What is the store's market niche? Beware the merchant who says, "I'm here to sell to everybody." Unless the owner has a clear idea of whom the store is directed toward, and what services and advertising are appropriate for that target, there will be a lot of money lost identifying those elements.
5. Who has been consulted for advice? Beware the 'Lone Ranger.' A successful business person knows the importance of developing a support team.

New tenants are definitely not equal. By carefully analyzing a store's survival risk and redirecting some of the shopping center's money toward the development of an incubator—money normally spent on tenant improvements and leasing commissions resulting from high turnover—the center could well finish financially ahead. In today's market the center is in business *with* its merchants, therefore directing resources that promote success toward them makes good economic sense.

Betty Konarski has spent 15 years as retail store owner and shopping center manager. She is currently dividing her time between consulting with mall developers in Washington and Oregon and supervising the Small Business Institute at Seattle University, Seattle, Washington.

Quality Circles

• Jane A. Secola, CMD, Enterprise Development Co.

The success of a shopping center project depends on the success of its individual retailers. Indeed, the selection and nurturing of merchants is today's biggest marketing challenge. The idea of motivating merchants to increase sales is not new. It finds its roots in the somewhat controlled environment and the concept of percentage rent participation.

Many of our merchants tend to be first-time and/or minority retailers. The small, special merchant contributes to the flavor, color, and variety of the center—providing a unique ambience that attracts customers but requires individual and special attention. Similar care can be applied to larger, more traditional merchants.

At Enterprise Development Co., the merchant motivation program is designed to challenge all retailers and to provide special individual attention. The objectives are:

1. To increase sales and therefore profits and percentage rents.
2. To identify merchants who will probably not succeed for reasons beyond control and to recommend releasing efforts early enough to cut losses.
3. To provide opportunities for new merchants who can contribute to the overall success of the center.

Our merchant motivation plan encompasses various means in the pursuit of the above objectives, namely:

• Work-study groups
• Individual counseling
• Merchant advisers
• Quality circles
• Seminars and "universities"
• Other continuing education opportunities.

Quality circles were originally pioneered by the Japanese and then picked up and emulated throughout the world by countless organizations to help foster new ideas, enthusiasm, and success in the workplace. We have adapted the quality circle management technique to the shopping center milieu, in the hope of further involving merchants in the marketing process.

Quality circles do not devise the marketing plan for the center. Their function is to work within an overall plan and make it more effective for each store.

The technique draws employees from all levels of the corporate structure to participate in discussion groups whose purpose is to critique, plan, and implement new procedures designed to make the company achieve higher levels of productivity.

Merchants are divided into groups of 10 to 12 according to center "neighborhoods," that is, merchants whose stores are located near one another. At a general meeting, all the groups are informed of the company's marketing program for the year. The groups then meet separately to develop their own marketing ideas to tie in to the planned events or marketing flights planned by center management.

Planned meetings begin two or three months before each event, although groups meet on a regular monthly basis. Group leaders confer with their center's marketing director to help coordinate all efforts. Once every quarter all groups come together for a general meeting. Here they explain what has been done so far and what they are planning to do in coming months. The exchange of ideas contributes to a competitive spirit.

Other aspects of our merchant motivation plan tie in well with quality circles and boost merchant morale. Seminars and "universities" held prior to an opening, expansion, or revitalization are especially effective because they involve all persons whose goal is to produce a successful store—managers, employees, owners, advertising agencies, and so on—and encourage creative thinking in a "family" atmosphere.

Among the topics addressed by experts are: retailing,

display, finance, cash flow, food handling, accounting, inventory, buying, personnel, selling, service, merchandising, and management.

Merchants with various interests generally meet for the first time at a "university" or seminar before going on to meet in their quality circle group. Discussion subjects are assigned, such as:

- How do you plan to capture the customers who attend the grand opening and attract them into your store?
- What will you do to reach the office workers in the surrounding area?
- How can you capitalize on the conventions and tourism in your market area this year?
- What do you plan to do for the holiday season to bring more customers into your stores?
- How will you help make the spring sale creditable and desirable in the market?

Then, deadlines are set, after which retailers plot their own activities.

Implementation of the motivation plan begins in the preopening stage and continues once the center is in business. A merchant adviser or marketing director responsible for the plan keeps records and evaluations of each merchant through sales analysis and works closely with the center's general manager. The person responsible for the plan should meet with the general manager and director of property operations to determine problems and opportunities. From time to time it may be a good idea for the adviser to:

- Work behind the counter to demonstrate sales techniques.
- Help locate display items.
- Go on buying trips with the merchant.
- Suggest time-saving methods.
- Help with merchandise presentations.
- Help with employee training.

Implementation might range from a suggestion for a new recipe for food, a packaging system, or an advertising idea, to a change in the merchant's use clause. The effort continues until the merchant is operating a profitable business in a serviceable manner.

The quality circle could become the primary method for providing most of the new ideas and much of the marketing energy in the future, while the merchants' association and marketing fund assume a supervisory role. Today, many good marketing ideas are not being implemented effectively because individual merchants have been participating on a limited basis in the aggregate marketing program. Quality circles could become the method whereby center management and merchants pursue their common goal of productivity.

Jane A. Secola, CMD, past member of the International Council of Shopping Centers' Certified Marketing Director Committee, was project coordinator for the first public service program offered by the International Council of Shopping Centers (ICSC), the KIDS program in 1986. She has spoken at many ICSC panels and workshops, and is the winner of many ICSC awards, including the first MAXI award for merchant motivation with the quality circle concept. She is presently working as a marketing specialist and strategist for retail shopping centers.

9
Resources

This chapter provides you with resources for additional information and assistance on retailing. It includes retail consultants, trade organizations, publications, audiovisuals, meetings, conventions and trade shows. This is not an exhaustive listing, therefore those resources listed should only be considered as helpful suggestions. You, or an otherwise qualified person at your company, should review and determine which ones are appropriate for your retail tenant. The International Council of Shopping Centers does not recommend or endorse any product or vendor listed here. Add to these suggestions as you hear about additional resources to the retail trade from your colleagues and through retail-oriented publications and meetings.

ORGANIZATIONS

American Marketing Association
250 South Wacker Drive, Chicago, Illinois 60606; (312) 648-0536

Direct Marketing Association
6 East 43rd Street, New York, New York 10017; (212) 689-4977

Illuminating Engineers Society of North America
345 East 47th Street, New York, New York 10017; (212) 705-7926

Institute of Store Planners
25 North Broadway, Tarrytown, New York 10591; (914) 332-1806

International Association of Business Communicators (IABC)
870 Market Street, San Francisco, California 94102; (415) 433-3400

International Council of Shopping Centers
665 Fifth Avenue, New York, New York 10022; (212) 421-8181

Marketing Research Association
111 East Wacker Drive, Chicago, Illinois 60601; (312) 644-6610

National Electric and Nonelectric Signs Association
801 North Fairfax Street, Suite 205, Alexandria, Virginia 22314; (703) 836-4012

National Retail Merchants Association
100 West 31st Street, New York, New York 10001; (212) 244-8780

Point of Purchase Advertising Institute
66 North Van Brunt Street, Englewood, New Jersey 07630; (201) 585-8400

Retail Advertising Conference
67 East Oak Street, Chicago, Illinois 60611; (312) 280-9344

Retail Council of Canada
210 Dundas Street, Suite 600, Toronto, Ontario M5G 2E8; (416) 598-4684

Western Association of Visual Merchandise (WAVM)
27 Scott Street, San Francisco, California 94117; (415) 431-1234

PUBLICATIONS

Periodicals

Advertising Age
Crain Communications, Inc., 1400 Woodbridge Avenue, New York, New York 10017; (212) 210-0100. Includes news and features related to advertising and marketing in the U.S. and overseas.

American Demographics
P.O. Box 68, Ithaca, New York 14850; (607) 273-6343. Business magazine of demographic trends, sources, and techniques.

Chain Merchandiser
65 Crocker Avenue, Piedmont, California 94611; (415) 547-4545. Improving merchandising methods at every level of the marketing and distributing process.

Chain Store Age
Lebhar-Friedman, 425 Park Avenue, New York, New York 10022; (212) 371-9400. Merchandise information, operating techniques, training material, and industry news for headquarters executives and store managers.

Discount Store News
Lebhar-Friedman, 425 Park Avenue, New York, New York 10022; (212) 371-9400. Information on planning, merchandising, and operating discount stores. Spot news and feature reports on developments in the discount store field.

Electronics Merchandising
CES Publishing Corporation, 345 Park Avenue South, New York, New York 10010; (212) 686-7744. Informs retailers and salespeople on how to improve sales via store display and merchandise.

Home Furnishings Daily
Fairchild Publications, 7 East 12th Street, New York, New York 10003; (212) 741-4000. Covers the news of the home products industry.

Mark McCormack's Success Secrets
One Erieview Plaza, Suite 1300, Cleveland, Ohio 44114; (216) 522-1200. Offers techniques for improving managerial skills and performance.

Marketing News
American Marketing Association, 250 South Wacker Drive, Suite 200, Chicago, Illinois 60606; (312) 648-0536. Current articles on marketing and association activities.

Men's Ad Review
Retail Reporting Corporation, 101 Fifth Avenue, New York, New York 10003; (212) 255-9595. Ideas for advertising by specialty types; includes recent effective ads in bimonthly bulletin.

NRMA Ad Pro
National Retail Merchants Association, 100 West 31st Street, New York, New York 10001; (212) 244-8780. In-depth analysis of selected advertising programs, including special events.

Profitable Retailer
514 Fort Worth Club Building, Fort Worth, Texas 76102; (817) 731-1491. Instructions for small and medium-sized retailers.

Retail Advertising Week
Retail Reporting Bureau, 101 Fifth Avenue, New York, New York 10003; (212) 255-9595. For department and specialty stores, advertising agencies, television stations.

Roper's: The Public Pulse
The Roper Organization Inc., 205 East 42nd Street, New York, New York 10017; (212) 599-0700. A monthly report on what Americans are thinking, doing, and buying.

Sales and Marketing Digest
Devonshire Financial Corp., 527 Third Avenue, Suite 312, New York, New York 10016-9991; (800) 231-2310. A wide-ranging selection of articles from various publications on topics of interest to sales and marketing professionals.

Sales and Marketing Management

Billboard Communications, 633 Third Avenue, New York, New York 10017; (212) 986-4800. Directed at executives responsible for managing sales and marketing functions in their organizations.

Signs of the Times

407 Gilbert Avenue, Cincinnati, Ohio 45202; (513) 421-2050. The sign field, including electric, illuminated signs, and outdoor advertising.

Specialty Store Service Bulletin

Vanguard Publications, P.O. Box 17123, Lansing, Michigan 48901; (517) 371-5550. Women's apparel store management aids: advertising, merchandising, promoting.

Store Planning Service

Retail Reporting Bureau, 101 Fifth Avenue, New York, New York 10003; (212) 255-9595. Color photographs showing interiors, departments, fixtures of newly opened American stores.

Stores

National Retail Merchants Association, 100 West 31st Street, New York, New York 10001; (212) 244-8780. For retail executives whose responsibilities include areas of merchandising, financing; delineates and interprets strategies and tactics.

Views and Reviews

Retail Reporting Bureau, 101 Fifth Avenue, New York, New York 10003; (212) 255-9595. Supplies color photographs of leading window displays.

Visual Merchandising and Store Design

Signs of the Times Publications, 407 Gilbert Street, Cincinnati, Ohio 45202; (513) 421-2050. Articles for visual merchandising in the field of retail marketing.

Volume Retail Merchandising

Canadian Engineering Publications, 111 Peter Street, Suite 411, Toronto, Ontario M5V 2W2; (416) 596-1642. New products, trends, useful statistics, people, promotion, and news, pointing the way to more profitable retailing and merchandising.

W

Fairchild Publications, 7 East 12th Street, New York, New York 10003; (212) 741-4000. General publication with good coverage of women's fashions.

Women's Wear Daily

Fairchild Publications, 7 East 12th Street, New York, New York 10003; (212) 741-4000. Retail trade publication covering women's and children's apparel, accessories, and cosmetics.

Books

Advertising, 5th Ed.

by John S. Wright, Daniel S. Warner, Willis L. Winter Jr. McGraw-Hill, Inc., 1221 Avenue of the Americas, New York, New York 10020; (212) 512-2000.

Annual Christmas Planning and Idea Workbook

National Retail Merchants Association, 100 West 31st Street, New York, New York 10001; (212) 244-8780.

The Best in Ad Sales

Retail Reporting, 101 Fifth Avenue, New York, New York 10003; (212) 255-9595.

The Best of New York's Shop Windows

Retail Reporting, 101 Fifth Avenue, New York, New York 10003; (212) 255-9595.

Boosting Employee Performance Through Better Motivation

National Retail Merchants Association, 100 West 31st Street, New York, New York 10001; (212) 244-8780.

The Buyer's Manual

National Retail Merchants Association, 100 West 31st Street, New York, New York 10001; (212) 244-8780.

Communicating When Your Company is Under Siege
by Marion K. Pinsdorf. Lexington Books, 125 Spring Street, Lexington, Massachusetts 02173; (617) 860-1208.

Creative Markdown Practices for Profit
Fairchild Books and Visuals, 7 East 12th Street, New York, New York 10003; (212) 741-5814.

Data Service
Sales and Marketing Management, Billboard Publications, 633 Third Avenue, New York, New York 10017; (212) 984-2314. Has in-depth demographic data on all state counties in the United States, figures on disposable income, population demographics, market rankings and characteristics.

Developing a Winning Marketing Plan
by William A. Cohen. John Wiley & Sons, Inc., 605 Third Avenue, New York, New York 10158-0012; (212) 850-6791.

Direct Mail Advertising and Selling for Retailers
National Retail Merchants Association, 100 West 31st Street, New York, New York 10001; (212) 244-8780.

Direct Marketing Success: What Works and Why
by Freeman F. Gosden Jr. John Wiley & Sons, Inc., 605 Third Avenue, New York, New York 10158-0012; (212) 850-6791.

Dollars and Cents of Shopping Centers
Urban Land Institute, 1090 Vermont Avenue NW, Washington, D.C. 20005; (202) 289-8500. Average rents, sizes, percentage leases, sales per square foot, etc., for retailers in shopping centers, by shopping center type and region of the United States.

Effective Public Relations, 6th Ed.
by Scott M. Cutlip and Allen H. Center. Prentice Hall, Route 9W, Englewood Cliffs, New Jersey 07632; (201) 592-2000.

Experts in Action: Inside Public Relations
by Bill Cantor and Chester Burger. Longman, Inc., 95 Church Street, White Plains, New York 10601; (914) 993-5000.

Fairchild's Book of Window Displays
Fairchild Books and Visuals, 7 East 12th Street, New York, New York 10003; (212) 741-5814.

Financial and Operating Results
National Retail Merchants Association, 100 West 31st Street, New York, New York 10001; (212) 244-8780.

Fundamentals of Merchandise Presentation
by Robert Colborne. Signs of the Times Publishing Co., 407 Gilbert Avenue, Cincinnati, Ohio 45202; (800) 543-1925.

Guide to Member Services and Staff Specialists
National Retail Merchants Association, 100 West 31st Street, New York, New York 10001; (212) 244-8780.

Handbook of Demographics for Marketing and Advertising: Sources and Trends on the U.S. Consumer
by William Lazer. Lexington Books, 125 Spring Street, Lexington, Massachusetts 02173; (617) 860-1208.

Handbook of Promotions
by S. Ulanof. McGraw-Hill Book Company, 1221 Avenue of the Americas, New York, New York 10020; (212) 997-2271.

How to Produce a Fashion Show
Fairchild Books and Visuals, 7 East 12th Street, New York, New York 10003; (212) 741-5814.

How to Sell Fashion
Fairchild Books and Visuals, 7 East 12th Street, New York, New York 10003; (212) 741-5814.

Improving Apparel Shop Profits
National Retail Merchants Association, 100 West 31st Street, New York, New York 10001; (212) 244-8780.

Low-Cost Marketing Strategies: Field-Tested Techniques for Tight Budgets
by Elisabeth Deran. Greenwood Press, 88 Post Road West, Box 5007, Westport, Connecticut 08881; (203) 226-3571.

The Marketer's Guide to Media Vehicles, Methods and Options: A Sourcebook in Advertising and Promotion
by Ann Grossman. Greenwood Press, 88 Post Road West, Box 5007, Westport, Connecticut 08881; (203) 226-3571.

Media Math
by Robert W. Hall. National Textbook Co., 4255 West Touhy Avenue, Lincolnwood, Illinois 60646; (312) 679-5500.

Media Planning: A Practical Guide
by Jim Surmanek. National Textbook Co., 4255 West Touhy Avenue, Lincolnwood, Illinois 60646; (312) 679-5500.

Merchandise Control and Budgeting
National Retail Merchants Association, 100 West 31st Street, New York, New York 10001; (212) 244-8780.

Merchandising and Operating Results
National Retail Merchants Association, 100 West 31st Street, New York, New York 10001; (212) 244-8780.

National Benchmarks
Stillerman Jones and Company, Inc., 1728 East 86th Street, Indianapolis, Indiana 46240; (317) 844-4960. Summary of shopping center customer surveys that identifies traits and trends, average number of stores visited, time and money spent, etc. Annual.

The Practical Handbook and Guide to Focus Group Research
by Thomas L. Greenbaum. Lexington Books, 125 Spring Street, Lexington, Massachusetts 02173; (617) 860-1208.

Printing and Production for Promotional Materials
by Robert Woods. Van Nostrand Reinhold Company, Inc., 115 Fifth Avenue, New York, New York 10003; (212) 254-3232.

The Profitmaker for Small Stores
National Retail Merchants Association, 100 West 31st Street, New York, New York 10001; (212) 244-8780.

Public Relations in Action, 2nd Ed.
by Robert T. Reilly. Prentice Hall, Route 9W, Englewood Cliffs, New Jersey 07632; (201) 592-2000.

The Retail Advertising Manual
by Judy Young Ocko. Retail Reporting Bureau, 101 Fifth Avenue, New York, New York 10003; (212) 255-9595 or (800) 251-4545.

Retail Store Planning and Design Manual
National Retail Merchants Association, 100 West 31st Street, New York, New York 10001; (212) 244-8780.

Retailing Management, 5th Ed.
by William R. Davidson, Alton F. Doody, Daniel J. Sweeney. John Wiley & Sons, Inc., 605 Third Avenue, New York, New York 10158-0012; (212) 850-6791.

Sales and Marketing Magazine's Annual Survey of Buying Power
633 Third Avenue, New York, New York 10017; (212) 986-4800. Contains breakouts on estimated expenditures by merchandise category for each city, county, and state.

Shopping Center Operating Cost Analysis Report
International Council of Shopping Centers, 665 Fifth Avenue, New York, New York 10022; (212) 421-8181. Provides detailed data on actual shopping center operating costs and characteristics.

Shopping Centers and Malls
Retail Reporting, 101 Fifth Avenue, New York, New York 10003; (212) 255-9595.

Store Fronts and Facades
Retail Reporting, 101 Fifth Avenue, New York, New York 10003; (212) 255-9595.

Stores of the Year
Retail Reporting, 101 Fifth Avenue, New York, New York 10003; (212) 255-9595.

Store Windows That Sell
Retail Reporting, 101 Fifth Avenue, New York, New York 10003; (212) 255-9595.

Strategic Retail Marketing
Retail Council of Canada, 210 Dundas Street, Suite 600, Toronto, Ontario M5G 2E8; (416) 598-4684. A practical workbook guide to store sales and profit revitalization, as well as good basic information on how stores should operate.

United States Census Reports
United States Government Printing Office, Washington, D.C. 20402; (202) 783-3238. *Census of Population and Housing,* taken every ten years, gives demographic information according to geographic area; *Census of Retail Trade,* taken every five years, gives the number of establishments, sales, and employment by state and county; *Current Business Reports* come out monthly and give retail sales by category and location.

Visual Merchandising
National Retail Merchants Association, 100 West 31st Street, New York, New York 10001; (212) 244-8780.

Why They Buy: American Consumers Inside and Out
by Robert B. Settle and Pamela L. Alreck. John Wiley & Sons, Inc., 605 Third Avenue, New York, New York 10158-0012; (212) 850-6791.

Catalogs

A Catalog of Books, Films, and Periodicals
National Retail Merchants Association, 100 West 31st Street, New York, New York 10001; (212) 244-8780. Topics include merchandising and sales promotion and marketing.

Fairchild Books and Visuals Catalog
Fairchild Books and Visuals, 7 East 12th Street, New York, New York 10003; (212) 741-5814. Includes publications and videotapes covering such topics as Fashion Merchandising

and "Retailing, Merchandising, Marketing" from the publisher of *Women's Wear Daily.*

International Council of Shopping Centers Publications Catalog
ICSC Publications, 665 Fifth Avenue, New York, New York 10022; (212) 421-8181. Offers books, reports, and cassettes on shopping center management, marketing, retailing, leasing, and development.

AUDIOVISUAL MATERIAL

Database Marketing I and II
Direct Marketing Association, 6 East 43rd Street, New York, New York 10017; (212) 689-4977. Part I introduces database marketing to direct marketing professional; and part II goes into qualitative methods and advanced applications for analysts, researchers, and experienced marketing managers.

Direct Marketing Fundamentals
Direct Marketing Association, 6 East 43rd Street, New York, New York 10017; (212) 689-4977. For anyone who could benefit from better understanding direct marketing.

Trends in Interior Displays
Retail Reporting Corporation, 101 Fifth Avenue, New York, New York 10003; (212) 255-9595.

Up-Front Series: How to Deal with Employee Theft and Pilferage
National Retail Merchants Association, 100 West 31st Street, New York, New York 10001; (212) 244-8780.

Window Displays That Sell
Retail Reporting Corporation, 101 Fifth Avenue, New York, New York 10003; (212) 255-9595.

MEETINGS/CONVENTIONS/TRADE SHOWS

Direct Marketing Association
6 East 43rd Street, New York, New York 10017; (212) 689-4977. Annual exhibition and convention in October: Atlanta, 1988; Washington, DC, 1989. Exhibits and conferences dealing with retail advertising.

Illuminating Engineers Society of North America
345 East 47th Street, New York, New York 10017; (212) 705-7926. Annual convention in August: Minneapolis, 1988; Orlando, FL, 1989. Information by designers and architects on current trends in lighting, plus displays.

International Association of Business Communicators (IABC)
870 Market Street, San Francisco, California 94102; (415) 433-3400. Major convention in June for internal and external business communicators.

International Council of Shopping Centers
665 Fifth Avenue, New York, New York 10022; (212) 421-8181. Annual Spring convention in May. More than 70 meetings, conventions, and trade shows held throughout the year on shopping centers, including exhibitions, deal making sessions, discussions, seminars, and committee presentations.

National Association of Display Industries
468 Park Avenue South, New York, New York 10016-6820; (212) 213-2662. Trade show of display pieces held biannually in New York in June and December.

National Electric and Nonelectric Signs Association
801 North Fairfax Street, Suite 205, Alexandria, Virginia 22314; (703) 836-4012. Annual convention in April: San Francisco, 1989; San Antonio, TX, 1990. Trade show with exhibitions, conferences and discussions on signage.

National Retail Merchants Association/National Association of Display Industries

468 Park Avenue South, New York, New York 10016-6820; (212) 213-2662. (See next listing for NRMA address.) NRMA visual merchandising seminar followed by NADI display exhibition is held biannually in New York in June and December.

National Retail Merchants Association

100 West 31st Street, New York, New York 10001; (212) 244-8780. Annual convention in New York in January. General sessions on emerging issues and functional sessions on individual aspects of retailing.

Point of Purchase Advertising Institute

66 North Van Brunt Street, Englewood, New Jersey 07630; (201) 585-8400. Trade show in November, alternates between Chicago and New York: Chicago, 1988; New York, 1989.

Retail Council of Canada

210 Dundas Street, Suite 600, Toronto, Ontario M5G 2E8; (416) 598-4684. Annual conferences on general and marketing topics, plus a wide range of personal development workshops and seminars.

Western Association of Visual Merchandisers

27 Scott Street, San Francisco, California 94117; (415) 431-1234. March trade show in San Francisco. Includes list of exhibitors.

TENANT SERVICES/MOTIVATION CONSULTANTS

This listing was selected from the International Council of Shopping Centers' *Associate Member Survey of Products and Services*, which is updated annually from questionnaires mailed to ICSC associate member companies. As the topics covered by this book include merchant motivation, shopping center productivity, sales training, merchandising, and merchant education, an attempt was made to include only those firms that listed one or more of these areas in their description.

Dooley Retail Network

P.O. Box 11721, Indianapolis, Indiana 46201; (317) 266-9710. Provides merchant education, motivation, communication, participation and evaluation programs. Secret shopper reports. Tenant mix review, store merchandising/operations reviews, troubled merchant consulting, food court merchandising.

James Posner Associates

30 Park Avenue, New York, New York 10016; (212) 686-2749. Provides retail consulting services emphasizing the improvement of retail sales and shopping center productivity through improved tenant mix and retail skills.

Krown Development Associates

20 West 85th Street, New York, New York 10024; (212) 595-9723. Work with senior management to diagnose problems and implement customized training programs to aid employees and improve accountability.

R.M. Consultants Inc.

6065 Roswell Road, Suite 3123, Atlanta, Georgia 30328; (404) 252-5642. Help identify and resolve problems, evaluate tenant mix, and select location. Also, provide market analyses, feasibility studies and evaluation of competition.

R.G. Foster Associates Inc.

1500 Lafayette Street, Gretna, Louisiana 70053; (504) 368-7200. Provide audits of: tenant sales, construction contracts, operations, merchant associations, parking garages, ground leases, due diligence and income verifications.

Retail Consultants Inc.

374 Millburn Avenue, Millburn, New Jersey 07041; (201) 376-2020. Retail specialists with extensive experience in

marketing, merchandising, advertising/sales promotion, sales training, food courts, design. Work with financial institutions, developers and property managers in evaluating and improving shopping centers.

Sains Associates

1640 E. 50th Street, Chicago, Illinois 60615; (312) 667-6186. Retailing consultants providing merchant education and motivational seminars in retail salesmanship, management skills development, merchandise presentation, retailing strategies and one-on-one consultations to increase revenue.

Scott Sorensen Resources Inc.

535 Merle Hay Tower, Des Moines, Iowa 50310; (515) 276-7051. Provides seminars, workshops, customized presentations and business consultations on sales, marketing, and management/operations.

Very Special Events

11717 Bernardo Plaza Court, Suite 200, San Diego, California 92128; (619) 485-1171. Provides consultation and training programs in marketing, public relations, crisis management for developers and tenants. Also creates and produces national sponsored events for malls, coordinates mall grand openings and represents temporary tenants.